W9-CTG-974

Parent Tips

Set Realistic, Suitable Goals

At the start of each week, motivate your child to take ownership of their learning by having them set one or two goals. Then develop a shortlist of activities, exercises, and tasks to accomplish. Be sure that the activities are appropriate, and those agreed-upon goals are realistic.

Establish a Consistent Study Place and Time

Set aside 20 minutes, preferably around the same time each day. This will help your child to develop a routine.

Designate a Quiet Study Space

Make sure the study space is well lit and free from big distractions such as a television. Try to keep interruptions to a minimum by keeping cell phone ringers off.

Provide Necessary Learning Tools

Be ready for learning by having writing tools, art supplies, and paper at your child's fingertips.

Come Up with a Fun Name

Come up with a positive name for working on skills, such as "Brain Stretch Time," "Brain Booster," or "Brain Aerobics." By doing so, your child will view it as something beneficial and fun.

Give Effective Praise

Give specific praise for your child's efforts and the process. By giving genuine praise and constructive feedback about their performance and efforts, you're teaching your child to link their successes with the strategies and steps they're developing. This will ultimately encourage your child to see themselves as capable and confident learners.

Here are some examples!

I like the way you...
I noticed that you...
Tell me how you...

thought
used
explored
created
decided
chose

Always focus on their progress!

Instead of "Good job!"
Try "I like the way you kept trying even when you were frustrated."
Try "I like the way you check your work!"

Encouraging a Growth Mindset

The research of psychologist Dr. Carol Dweck tells us that people have two possible mindsets—a fixed mindset or a growth mindset. People with a fixed mindset believe that they are either smart or good at something, or they are not—and nothing can change that. People with a growth mindset believe that it is always possible to get better at doing something. Dr. Dweck has found that children with a growth mindset are more motivated to learn and achieve more than children with a fixed mindset.

How can you help children develop a growth mindset?

Talk about the brain: Explain that the brain becomes stronger by working hard to master new skills. Just as exercise makes muscles stronger, working at challenging thinking tasks makes the brain stronger.

View mistakes as learning opportunities: Let your child know that mistakes are valuable ways of learning where the problems lie. By carefully looking at mistakes, you and your child can learn where there are misunderstandings or missing pieces of knowledge. Mistakes pave the way to success!

Teach ways of dealing with frustration: Children can "turn off" when they become frustrated, which makes learning impossible. Teach your child ways to overcome frustration. For example, use the Internet to learn about breathing techniques that combat stress. You can also remind your child of skills that they have mastered in the past (such as learning to tie shoelaces) that took time and effort to learn.

Focus on praising the process: While it's fine to praise your child or the results they achieved, you can encourage a growth mindset by focusing your praise on the process. For example, praise your child's willingness to keep trying and their use of effective learning strategies, such as asking questions.

Model a growth mindset: Look for opportunities to reinforce with your child how to see things from a growth mindset. For example:

If your child says...	Respond by saying...
I'll never get this!	Maybe you can't do it yet, but you'll get better if you keep trying.
I've been working at this for a long time and I'm still not getting it right.	Look at these areas where you've made progress. Keep working and you'll make more progress.
Hey, I can finally do this!	Let's think about how you achieved success. Some of the things you did this time might help you with the next challenge.

Independent Reading Rubric

	Not Yet Meeting Expectations	Approaching Expectations	Meeting Expectations	Exceeding Expectations
Choice of Reading Level	Chooses reading materials they have read many times before, or which are below their reading level.	Chooses reading materials they have read once before, but are close to their reading level.	Chooses reading materials they have not read before, which are slightly below or at their reading level.	Chooses reading materials they have not read before, which are at or above grade level.
Choice of Genre • *Stories* • *Books* • *Magazines* • *Poetry* • *Graphic Novels*	Resists trying different types of reading materials.	Sometimes chooses different types of reading materials.	Usually chooses a variety of types of reading materials.	Consistently chooses a variety of types of reading materials.
Overall Attitude	Shows very little interest in reading.	Sometimes shows interest in reading.	Shows enthusiasm in reading.	Shows excitement in reading.

Oral Reading Rubric

	Not Yet Meeting Expectations	Approaching Expectations	Meeting Expectations	Exceeding Expectations
Expression and Flow	Rarely reads with expression or flow. Attention to punctuation is inconsistent and requires teacher prompts.	Sometimes reads with expression and flow. Attention to punctuation is inconsistent.	Usually reads with expression. Flow and pace of reading are mostly consistent. Attention to punctuation is usually consistent.	Consistently reads with expression. Flow and pace of reading are fluid. Attention to punctuation is always consistent.
Reading Strategies • *Look for other words with the same sound* • *Look for known parts of words* • *Use syllables to break the word into parts* • *Use context clues from the reading*	Rarely uses strategies to decode text. Makes several errors and needs teacher prompts to correct errors that interfere with meaning.	Uses some strategies to decode text. Makes some errors and sometimes self-corrects for meaning.	Usually uses various strategies to decode text. Makes few errors and usually self-corrects for meaning.	Independently uses various strategies to decode text. Makes minimal errors and almost always self-corrects for meaning.

Text Features

Text features help the reader to understand the text better. Here is a list of text features with a brief explanation on how they help the reader. Find an example of each text feature.

	Text Feature	Example
Table of Contents	Here the reader will find a list that provides the page numbers of the contents of the text.	
Heading	Here the reader will find a title that lets the reader know what the section is about.	
Glossary	Here the reader will find a list of words that have definitions of what they mean and how to say them.	
Diagram and Illustration	A diagram is an image that shows the parts of something. An illustration shows a drawing of an object.	
Label	A label tells the reader the title of a map, a diagram, or an illustration. Labels also draw attention to the details of an illustration or diagram.	
Caption	Captions are words that are placed below the illustrations. Captions give the reader more information about the map, diagram, or illustration.	
Map	Maps help the reader understand where something is happening. It is a visual representation of a location.	
Fact Box	A fact box gives the reader extra information about the topic.	

Reading Comprehension Checklist

Help your child develop and reinforce essential reading comprehension skills.

Before Reading – Make Predictions

☐ What do you think the story/text will be about? Look at the cover and think about the title.

While Reading – Check for Understanding

Author's Purpose

☐ Is the author trying to persuade, inform, or entertain the reader? How do you know?

☐ What is the genre of the reading/story/text?

☐ What message did the author want the reader to take away after reading the story/text?

☐ Why do you think the author chose the time and setting for the story/text?

☐ Was _____ a good title for the story/text? Why or why not?

Story Structure

☐ Is this text fact or fiction?

☐ What is this story/text mostly about?

☐ Where does this story/text take place?

☐ From whose point of view is the story/text told? How do you know?

☐ Who are the characters? How are they important to the story/text?

☐ In your opinion, could the characters exist in real life? Explain your thinking.

☐ What incident, situation, or problem occurred at the beginning of the story/text to get the story started?

☐ What is the problem/conflict in the story/text? How is it resolved?

☐ Did the author give clues about the outcome of the story/text? Explain your thinking and give examples.

☐ In order, list the major events of the story/text.

☐ What is the mood or feeling in the story/text? Give examples from the story/text of how the author created this mood or feeling.

☐ How does the author create suspense so that the reader wants to continue reading? Explain your thinking with examples.

Reading Comprehension Checklist

After Reading – Responding to the Text

- ☐ If you could give this story/text another title, what would it be?
- ☐ Retell the story/text in your own words.
- ☐ What happened in the beginning/middle/end of the story/text?
- ☐ Who is your favourite character?
- ☐ Which parts of the story/text could or could not happen in real life?
- ☐ Did you like the ending of the story? Tell why.
- ☐ What do you still wonder about after reading the story/text?
- ☐ What would you like to ask the author/one of the characters?
- ☐ What would you like to know more about?

Making Connections

- ☐ How does the text remind you about what you already know?

👤 Text-to-Self	📖 Text-to-Text	🌍 Text-to-World
How does this text relate to your own life?	How is this text similar to or different from something you have read before?	What does this text remind you of in the real world?

20 Book Reading Challenge

Colour each box as you finish reading the text. Add the title of the text.

a book of poetry	a fairy tale	a book that teaches a lesson about life	a historical fiction
a book that is part of a series	a book with suspense/mystery	a book that you read outside of class	a realistic fiction
a book that teaches you how to do something	a book with an adventure	a book recommended by a friend	a book that has become a movie
a non-fiction book	a fantasy	a biography	a graphic novel
a chapter book of your choice	a chapter book of your choice	a chapter book of your choice	a chapter book of your choice

Reading Comprehension Response

Title: _____

Choose a prompt from the reading comprehension skills checklist.

_____

Use details from the text to support your answer.

_____

_____

_____

_____

_____

_____

_____

_____

_____

R	**A**	**C**	**E**
Restate the question.	Answer the question.	Cite evidence.	Extend your thinking.
☐ Reword the question or prompt and turn it into a statement.	☐ Answer all parts of the question or prompt.	☐ Give evidence from the text to support your ideas or opinion. **For example:** • In the text... • For example... • On page___ it says... • The author writes... • According to the text... • I know this because...	☐ Make a connection to explain your thinking. **For example:** • This reminds me of... • This shows... • This proves... • I believe/feel... • Now I understand... • This is important because... • I can make a connection...

Reading Graphic Organizers

Graphic organizers are excellent tools to use for identifying and organizing information from a text into an easy-to-understand visual format. Students will expand their comprehension of a text as they complete the graphic organizers. Use these graphic organizers in addition to the activities in this book or with other texts.

Concept Web – Helps students understand the main idea of a text and how it is supported by key details.

Concept Map – Helps students gain a better understanding of how different subtopics within a text connect to the topic as a whole.

Venn Diagram/Comparison Chart – Helps students focus on the comparison of two items, such as individuals, ideas, events, or pieces of information. Students could compare by looking at which things are the same, or contrast by looking at which things are different.

Fact or Opinion – Helps students to distinguish between statements of fact and opinions. Facts are pieces of information that can be proven to be true. Opinions are pieces of information based on something that someone thinks or believes, but that cannot necessarily be proven to be true.

Cause and Effect – Helps students to recognize and explain relationships between events. The cause is the reason why an event happens, and the effect is the event that happens.

Context Clue Chart – Helps students organize clues that the author gives in a text to help define a difficult or unusual word. Encourage students to look for explanations of words within a text.

Drawing Conclusions and Making Inferences Chart – Helps students practise drawing conclusions and making inferences based on their prior knowledge, as well as what they read in the text.

Making Connections – Helps students to connect something they have read or experienced with the world around them.

A Concept Web For: _____

A **main idea** is what the text is mostly about. A **detail** is important information that tells more about the main idea. Pick a text and fill out the concept web.

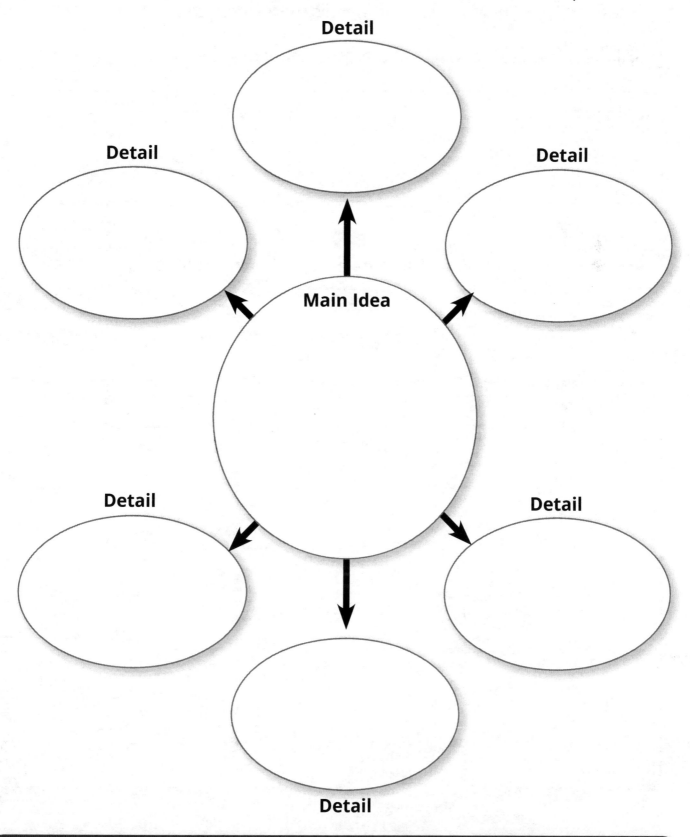

Detail

Detail

Detail

Main Idea

Detail

Detail

Detail

A Concept Map For:_____

A **main idea** is what the text is mostly about.
A **subheading** is the title given to a part of a text.
A **detail** is important information that tells more about the main idea.

Pick a non-fiction text and fill out the concept map.

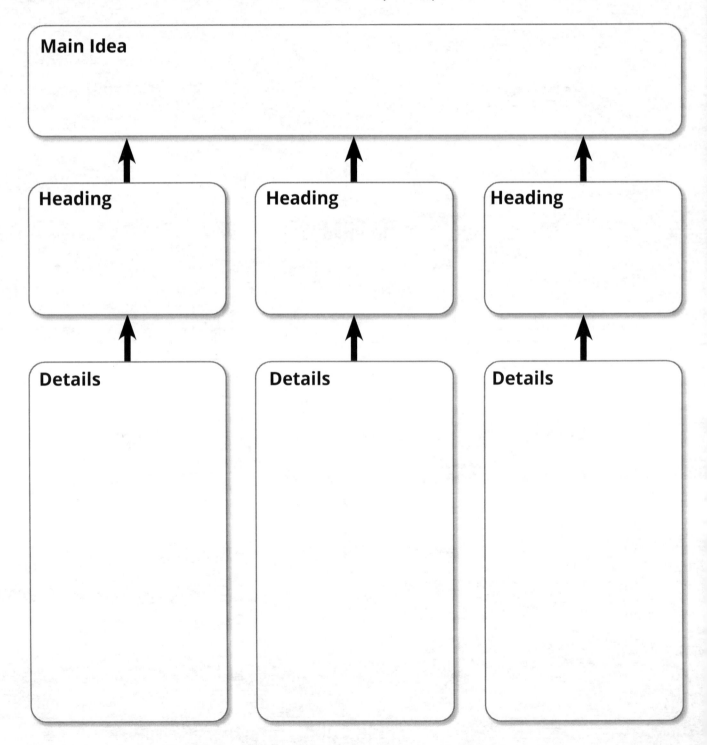

Main Idea

Heading

Heading

Heading

Details

Details

Details

A Venn Diagram About...

_____

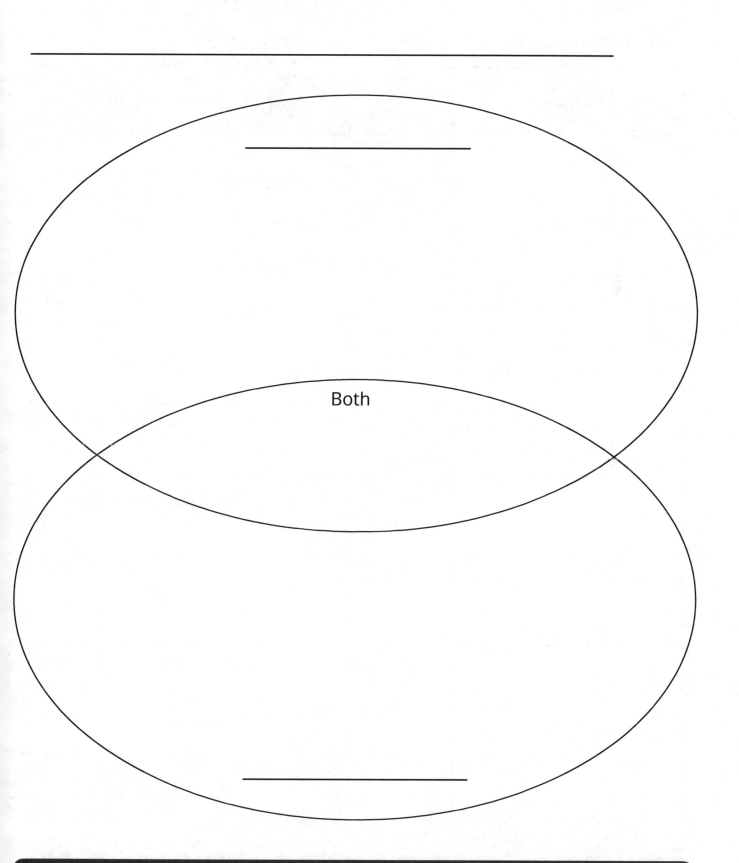

Both

Fact or Opinion

- ✓ **Facts** are statements that can be proven to be true.
- ☁ **Opinions** are feelings or beliefs about something.

Topic	Fact or Opinion?	How do you know?

Cause and Effect

Title: _____

- The **cause** is the reason something happens.
- The **effect** is what happens.

Cause

Effect

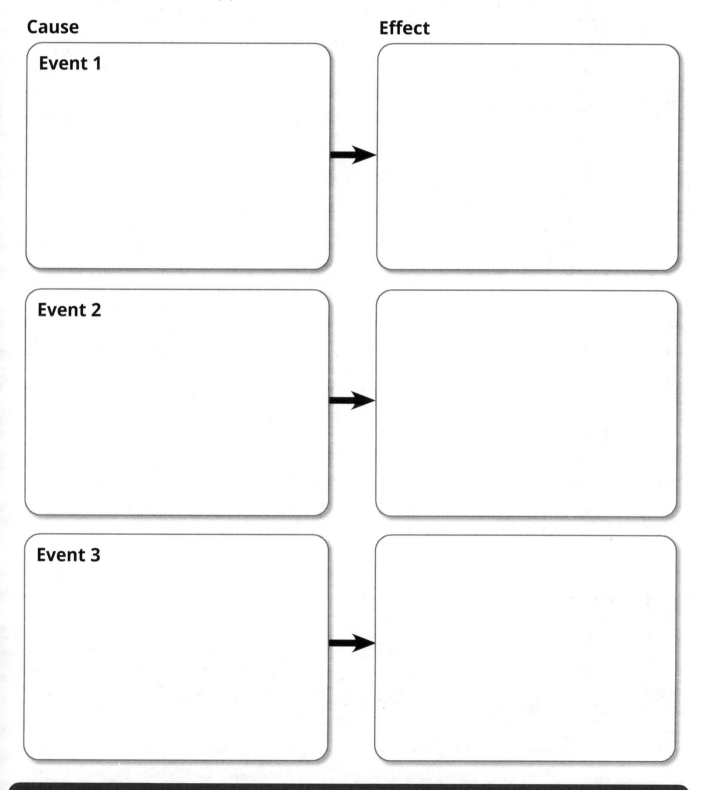

Event 1

Event 2

Event 3

Context Clue Chart

Context clues are hints that the author gives in a text that can help you find the meaning of a word.

Word	Context Clue from Text	Meaning of the Word

Drawing Conclusions and Making Inferences Chart

We make an **inference** when we combine what we know to be true with new information and come to a conclusion.

What I already know:	Clues from the text I read:	Help me to conclude or infer:

Comparing Books

Compare two books that you have read.
How are they the similar or different?

Compared to

_____   _____

Detailed information   Detailed information

Media Text Summary

Write a summary of a television program/online video you have watched.

Title: _____

Media text purpose: ☐ to inform   ☐ to entertain   ☐ to persuade

_____

_____

_____

_____

_____

_____

_____

_____

_____

_____

_____

_____

_____

_____

_____

_____

_____

Biography Snapshot

Subject of biography: _____

Early Life

_____
_____
_____
_____
_____
_____
_____

Adult Life

_____
_____
_____
_____
_____
_____
_____

Accomplishments

_____
_____
_____
_____
_____
_____
_____

Impact on Society

_____
_____
_____
_____
_____
_____
_____

Tracking Character Traits of...

Book Title: _____

A **character trait** is a way to describe someones personality.

Character

Character Trait	Character Trait	Character Trait

Evidence	Evidence	Evidence

Sample Character Traits

Admirable	Cheerful	Daring	Flexible	Helpful	Loyal	Responsible
Adventurous	Clever	Dedicated	Focused	Honest	Lucky	Sincere
Ambitious	Compassionate	Dependable	Friendly	Humble	Optimistic	Smart
Appreciative	Confident	Easygoing	Funny	Independent	Peaceful	Tasteful
Brave	Conscientious	Enthusiastic	Generous	Intelligent	Perseverant	Thoughtful
Calm	Courageous	Fair	Gentle	Kind	Persistent	Tolerant
Capable	Creative	Faithful	Gracious	Logical	Reliable	Trustworthy
Charming	Curious	Fearless	Hardworking	Loving	Respectful	Wise

Making Connections (text-to-text)

Learning Goal: I understand what I'm reading by making connections from the text to other texts I have read.

Choose a Sentence Starter:

☐ The text makes me think about...

☐ I made a connection from the text to another text when...

☐ An event from the text reminds me of another text because...

☐ Something in the text that has not happened in other texts I have read was...

☐ The character in the text is similar to or different from the character in...

☐ The text is similar to/different from another text where...

Consider:

- Genre
- Character
- Theme
- Setting
- Plot

Success Criteria

When explaining my connection:

☐ I will state the type of connection I am making to the text.

☐ I will state the idea from the text that made me think of the connection.

☐ I will support my connection with proof from the text and well-developed reasoning.

☐ I will organize and write my ideas in a way that is easy to read and understand.

☐ I will use transition words to connect my ideas clearly.

☐ I will check for correct spelling, punctuation, and grammar.

Learning Goal: I understand what I'm reading by making connections from the text to my own experiences.

Choose a Sentence Starter:

☐ The text makes me think about...

☐ I made a connection from the text to myself when...

☐ When ____ happened in the text, it reminded me of...

☐ When ____ happened in the text, it made me feel...

☐ After reading the text, my opinion changed/did not change because...

☐ If I were that character in the text, I would...

☐ The character in the text I can best relate to is...

☐ The text reminds me of similarities to/differences between:

- my life, family, and friends
- experiences I have had
- places I have been

Success Criteria

When explaining my connection:

☐ I will state the type of connection I am making to the text.

☐ I will state the idea from the text that made me think of the connection.

☐ I will support my connection with proof from the text and well-developed reasoning.

☐ I will organize and write my ideas in a way that is easy to read and understand.

☐ I will use transition words to connect my ideas clearly.

☐ I will check for correct spelling, punctuation, and grammar.

Making Connections (text-to-world)

Learning Goal: I can connect what I am reading to something that is happening, or something that has happened, in the world.

Choose a Sentence Starter:

☐ The text makes me think about....

☐ The text is like things or events that happen in the real world because...

☐ The text is different from things or events that happen in the real world because...

☐ Knowledge of the world around me helps me understand the text because...

☐ The text reminds me of similarities in/differences between:

- something I have seen or heard in the media
- historical events or current events

Success Criteria

When explaining my connection:

☐ I will state the type of connection I am making to the text.

☐ I will state the idea from the text that made me think of the connection.

☐ I will support my connection with proof from the text and well-developed reasoning.

☐ I will organize and write my ideas in a way that is easy to read and understand.

☐ I will use transition words to connect my ideas clearly.

☐ I will check for correct spelling, punctuation, and grammar.

That Reminds Me Of...

Title: _____

```
┌─────────────────────────────────────────┐
│                                         │
│                                         │
│                                         │
│                                         │
│                                         │
│                                         │
│                                         │
└─────────────────────────────────────────┘
```

This text reminds me of: 📖 text-to-text 👤 text-to-self 🌐 text-to-world

Let me tell you why.

_____

_____

_____

_____

_____

_____

_____

_____

_____

_____

_____

Under the surface of Earth there are huge slabs of rock. These slabs are called **tectonic plates**. These **plates** move very **slowly**. Tectonic plates can **rub** against each other as they move in **different directions**.

Sometimes, two tectonic plates get stuck as they rub against each other. **Force** builds up as the plates keep trying to move. Finally, there is enough force to make the plates move again. All the force that has built up makes the plates **move quickly** for a few moments. This movement causes the **surface of Earth** to **tremble** and **shake**. An earthquake is happening!

Think about a time when you had trouble unscrewing the lid of a jar. The lid and the top of the jar were stuck together. You used your hand to put more and more force on the jar lid to make it move. Finally, there was enough force to make the lid move. This example gives you an idea of how force builds up to make tectonic plates move after they have been stuck together.

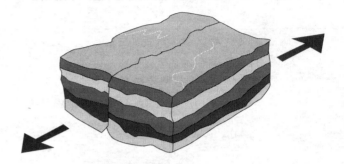

Force builds as two plates that are stuck keep trying to move.

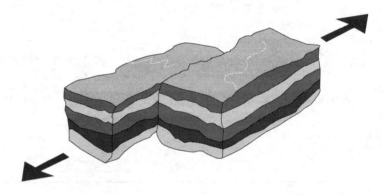

Finally, enough force builds up to make the plates move quickly.

How Earthquakes Affect People

Some earthquakes are more **powerful** than others. In some places, earthquakes happen often, but the earthquakes are very weak. These earthquakes make the ground tremble just a tiny bit. People in the area do not even notice that an earthquake has happened because they cannot feel the ground moving. These earthquakes do not cause any damage.

A powerful earthquake causes the ground to shake a lot. This shaking can cause a lot of **damage** to **buildings** and other **structures**, such as bridges. In places where earthquakes tend to happen often, there are rules for building new structures strong enough to stand up to most earthquakes. Many older structures were built before the rules were put in place. Often, the worst damage from an earthquake happens to older buildings.

"Earthquakes"-Think About It

1. What are *tectonic plates*?

_____

_____

2. The overall structure of this text is cause and effect. Complete the chart to show causes and effects in the text.

Cause	Effect
Two tectonic plates get stuck as they rub against each other.	
	The plates move quickly for a few moments.
The plates move quickly for a few moments.	
An earthquake is so weak that people do not notice it.	
	There is a lot of damage to buildings and other structures.

3. What is one step people have taken to try to prevent structures from getting damaged during an earthquake?

_____

_____

4. Why are many older structures often damaged in an earthquake?

_____

_____

A Truly Canadian Animal

The beaver has had a bigger **impact** on Canada's history and its **exploration** than any other animal or plant. No wonder it was chosen as a **symbol** of our country.

Built for the Water
The beaver is a **rodent**, like a mouse or rat. But the beaver is the largest rodent in North America. It is built to spend time **underwater**. Thanks to its thick fur and **waterproof** oil, even when a beaver has been **submerged** for several minutes, it is still not wet to the skin.

A beaver can close **valves** in its nostrils and ears when it dives underwater. This furry swimmer can even stop water from getting into its lungs.

Thick, Rich Fur
Beaver pelts were the most **valuable** furs in Europe during the 1600s. The best furs came from Canada. Europeans wanted the furs to make **beaver hats**—they were **status symbols** at the time. It is likely European countries would never have explored and fought over Canada if it were not for the beaver and its thick, rich fur.

When the **fur trade** started, scientists believe there were 6 million beavers living in what is now known as Canada. By the mid-1800s, when **fashions** in hats changed, the beaver was almost **extinct**. Since then, the beaver's numbers have slowly increased as Canadians realized how important this animal is.

Master Builders
Beavers build dams and lodges. That makes them one of the only **mammals**, besides humans, that can build their own **environment**. Beavers live in the lodges, which are dome-shaped and made of sticks and mud. The entrances to a lodge are underwater.

Beavers chew down small trees to build dams. These provide still, deep water to protect the colony's lodges from **predators**. Deep water also means the pond's bottom will not **freeze**, so the beavers will not be blocked in their lodge.

Without beaver dams, small streams would flow through forests and meadows without stopping. The dams cause ponds and marshes to form and many wild birds and animals depend on them.

1. What is the main idea of this text?

_____

_____

2. Lists ways the beaver changed Canada's history and ways it is changing its environment.

_____

_____

_____

_____

3. Read the text again, then write two other possible titles for it.

_____

_____

4. Imagine you are a beaver chewing down a tree. Write five sentences about the process.

_____

_____

_____

_____

_____

5. Choose another animal to be a symbol of Canada. Explain your choice.

_____

_____

_____

_____

_____

How Does That Fly?

What Forces Affect Airplanes?

Airplanes fly because of four **forces**. These forces are **weight**, **lift**, **thrust**, and **drag**.

- Weight is the force of **gravity** on the plane. Gravity wants to pull the plane down toward Earth.
- Lift is the force that acts to keep the plane up. Lift is created by the differences in **air pressure** below and above the wings of a plane.
- Thrust is the force that moves the plane **forward**. Engines of a plane produce thrust.
- Drag is the force that wants to pull the plane **backward**. Drag is caused by **friction** between the body of the plane and the air.

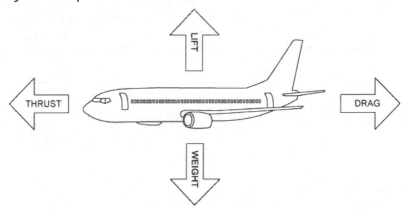

For an airplane to **take off**, the thrust must be greater than the drag, and the lift must be greater than the weight. For an airplane to land, the thrust must be less than the drag, and the lift must be less than the weight. When the airplane is **flying straight** and at an even level, thrust and drag are equal, and lift and weight are equal.

Bigger and Bigger Planes

Since the first flight in a powered, **controlled** airplane in 1903, planes have become bigger and bigger. The airplane that first made **air travel** popular and profitable was the Douglas DC-3. Introduced in 1936, this plane could carry 21 passengers and fly 2405 kilometres non-stop. Today, the Airbus A380 can carry 525 passengers and fly 15 700 kilometres non-stop. How can planes be so much bigger and still fly?

Bigger planes need engines that produce more speed. The invention of the **jet engine** allowed planes to fly faster and higher. **Commercial jet planes** started flying in the 1950s. Through the years, jet engines have become **more powerful** so planes can fly faster. They have also become more **fuel efficient**. The faster a plane can fly, the more lift it will have. But weight is still important, especially when the planes are bigger and they carry more passengers. Airplane makers have done many things to keep their planes as light as possible. The bodies of airplanes are being made of materials that are **lighter** and yet **strong**. Even seats are being made of lighter materials.

1. What does gravity want to do to an airplane? What does drag want to do? What two forces overcome gravity and drag so a plane can fly?

_____

_____

2. Which part of the text does the diagram relate to? Does the diagram help you understand the written information better? Why or why not?

_____

_____

_____

3. What happens to the forces when an airplane is flying level and straight?

_____

_____

4. One meaning of the word *efficient* is to use a product with the least waste or effort. What do you think the phrase "fuel efficient" means?

_____

_____

_____

5. Why are jet engines important for modern planes?

_____

_____

_____

6. What are the differences between the first passenger airplanes and the planes today?

_____

_____

_____

The Legacy of Terry Fox

A **legacy** is something that is left for others, usually by a person who has died. Terry Fox was a **hero** who left a legacy that has lasted more than 30 years. This legacy is still going strong.

Who Was Terry Fox?

Terry Fox was born in 1958 in Winnipeg, Manitoba, and was raised in Port Coquitlam, British Columbia. Terry found out he had **bone cancer** in one leg when he was 18 years old. He had to have his leg **amputated** above the knee. Before the operation, he read about an **amputee** who ran the **marathon** in New York City. He felt sorry for the other people in the hospital who had cancer—mostly the children. So he decided that he would run to raise money for **cancer research**.

Terry started **training** to run with his **artificial** leg. In April 1980, he started his Marathon of Hope. He planned to run across Canada, running a marathon every day. (A marathon is 40 kilometres.) He hoped his run would **inspire** people to give money for cancer research.

Terry started in St. John's, Newfoundland. He ran for 143 days, covering 5373 kilometres. But he had to stop because the cancer had returned. Terry fought hard against the cancer, but he died in June 1981.

The Terry Fox Run

Terry's Marathon of Hope raised $23 million for cancer research. Since then, the Terry Fox Run have been held every year. Before he died, Terry Fox planned with others how these runs would be organized.

The Terry Fox Run has no prizes. The run is for all people. Participants can run, walk, ride bicycles—even wear funny costumes. The run can be any length, but is usually 5 to 15 kilometres. No one has to pay to run. Participants try to get people to **sponsor** them. Most of this money goes directly to cancer research in Canada. The Terry Fox Run in Canada takes place every year on the second Sunday after Labour Day.

There is also a **National School Run Day** in Canada. Students and teachers from all across the country run to raise money. Some schools also hold bake sales or hockey games. These events take place on a day in September.

The Terry Fox Run has spread around the world. Some countries that have the Terry Fox Run are Argentina, India, Australia, Italy, and Japan. The Terry Fox Run is held in the United States from New York City to Los Angeles. The money raised by the runs usually goes to cancer research in that country. **International Terry Fox Runs** can take place on any date.

"The Legacy of Terry Fox"–Think About It

1. What is Terry Fox's legacy?

_____

_____

2. What does the word *amputated* mean? How do you know? What do you think an amputee is? Why?

_____

_____

_____

3. Why did Terry Fox decide to run to raise money for cancer research?

_____

_____

_____

4. What are two differences between the Terry Fox Run in Canada and International Terry Fox Runs?

_____

_____

_____

5. The author says that Terry Fox was a hero. What reasons does the author give to support this?

_____

_____

_____

The Teacher and the Thief

There was once a great teacher named Benzei. Children from far and wide came to study at Benzei's school. Benzei loved his students and promised to do everything possible to help each one of them learn.

One day, a new student named Taku came to the school. Shortly after that, things started to go missing. The other students suspected that Taku was stealing. They decided to watch him and see if he really was the thief.

Before long, the students caught Taku stealing a pen. They went to Benzei and told him what they had seen. Everyone expected that Benzei would expel Taku from the school. Benzei did nothing. Taku continued to come to school each day.

Soon, Taku was caught stealing again. The students went to Benzei. Still Benzei did nothing. Word of the thief at Benzei's school soon spread throughout the village.

"What is wrong with Benzei?" asked one parent. "How can he allow a thief to stay at the school?"

"He does not punish the thief for stealing," said another parent. "He is setting a bad example for our children. They should learn that if they steal, they should expect to be punished."

"Benzei is now an old man," said the village doctor. "Perhaps his mind is starting to go. We must keep an eye on him and see if he is still fit to teach the children."

One man spoke up to defend Benzei. "Benzei was my teacher when I was a child, and I still visit him once a week. I can assure you that Benzei's mind is as strong as ever. There must be a reason why he does not punish the thief. Let us wait and see."

Once again, Taku was caught stealing. One of the students drew up a petition saying that if Taku was not expelled from the school, all the students who signed the petition would leave and go to another school. Every student except Taku signed the petition. Everyone was sure that now, finally, Taku would be expelled from the school.

Two of the older students presented the petition to Benzei. Benzei asked all the students in the school to gather together.

"I am proud of the students who signed this petition," said Benzei. "I can see that you have learned your lessons well, and you know right from wrong. Any school would be glad to accept you. But what about the student who has not learned right from wrong? What school would keep him for long? If I do not teach him, no one will. That is why I have not asked him to leave. I want all my students to learn."

Taku burst into tears when he realized how much Benzei cared about him. Taku never stole again.

None of the other students left Benzei's school. They knew that they would never find a teacher who cared more for his students than Benzei.

"The Teacher and the Thief"-Think About It

1. The beginning of the story tells a promise that Benzei made to his students. Does Benzei keep his promise? Provide support for your answer.

_____

_____

2. Why did the students suspect that Taku was the person who was stealing?

_____

_____

3. What happens when a student is expelled from a school?

_____

_____

_____

4. Before Benzei gathers all the students together, the story gives a clue that he has a reason for not expelling Taku. What is the clue?

_____

_____

5. Why did the students believe that they would never find another teacher who would care more about them than Benzei?

_____

_____

_____

6. Benzei did not want to expel Taku. How else could Benzei have tried to deal with the problem of Taku's stealing?

_____

_____

_____

Writing Skills Checklist

Encourage your child to be a confident writer! Ask your child to help write out a grocery list, a thank you note, or other messages. These opportunities for writing will help your child develop a purpose for writing in their everyday life.

Developing and Organizing Content

- ☐ Identify the topic, purpose, and audience for a variety of writing forms

- ☐ Generate ideas about a potential topic, using a variety of strategies and resources

- ☐ Gather information to support ideas for writing in a variety of ways and/or from a variety of sources

- ☐ Identify and order main ideas and supporting details, using a variety of graphic organizers

Using Knowledge of Form and Style in Writing

- ☐ Write longer and more complex texts using a variety of forms

- ☐ Establish an appropriate voice in their writing, with a focus on using words and stylistic elements that convey a specific mood such as amusement

- ☐ Use sentences of different lengths and structures

- ☐ Identify their point of view and other possible points of view on the topic, and determine whether their information sufficiently supports their own view

- ☐ Use specific words and phrases to create an intended impression

- ☐ Produce revised, draft pieces of writing to meet identified criteria based on the expectations related to content, organization, style, and use of conventions

Language Conventions

- ☐ Confirm spellings and word meanings or word choice using a variety of resources appropriate for the purpose

- ☐ Use punctuation appropriately to help communicate their intended meaning

- ☐ Proofread and correct their writing using guidelines

Avoiding Sentence Fragments

A **complete sentence** has a complete subject and a complete predicate. A complete sentence tells who or what the subject is, and what the subject does or did. In the example below, the **complete subject** is in bold. The **complete predicate** is underlined.

Example: **This door** *squeaks loudly every time someone opens it.*

A **sentence fragment** is not a complete sentence. A sentence fragment is **missing** a complete subject, a complete predicate, or both. Look at the examples below.

Example: The man in the long black coat.

This is a **sentence fragment**. It contains a complete subject, but it is missing a complete predicate. The sentence fragment does not tell who the man is or what he is doing.

Example: **The man in the long black coat** *is waiting for the bus.*

This is a **complete sentence** because it has a complete subject (in bold) and a complete predicate (underlined).

Example: Ran all the way home without stopping to rest.

This is a **sentence fragment**. It contains a complete predicate, but it is missing a complete subject. The sentence fragment does not tell who ran all the way home.

Example: **My sister** *ran all the way home without stopping to rest.*

This is a **complete sentence** because it has a complete subject (in bold) and a complete predicate (underlined).

Example: Across the meadow and through the woods.

This is a **sentence fragment**. It is missing a complete subject that tells who or what the sentence is about. It is also missing a complete predicate because it does not tell what the subject is doing.

Example: **Two brown mice** *scurried across the meadow and through the woods.*

This is a **complete sentence** because it has a complete subject (in bold) and a complete predicate (underlined).

Remember to check your writing to make sure each sentence contains a **complete subject** and a **complete predicate**. Revise any sentence fragments you find to create complete sentences.

Avoiding Sentence Fragments

1. The **sentence fragments** below are missing a **complete subject**, a **complete predicate**, or **both**. For each sentence fragment, circle what is missing.

   a) Crept slowly through the long grass in the field.

      complete subject   complete predicate   both are missing

   b) The people at the concert last night.

      complete subject   complete predicate   both are missing

   c) Behind the bookshelf near the window.

      complete subject   complete predicate   both are missing

   d) The boy in the corner with red hair and freckles.

      complete subject   complete predicate   both are missing

   e) As quickly as possible.

      complete subject   complete predicate   both are missing

   f) Suddenly tipped over and crashed to the floor.

      complete subject   complete predicate   both are missing

2. Beside each sentence below, write *CS* if it is a **complete sentence** or *SF* if it is a **sentence fragment**.

   a) Some of the players were nervous before the championship game. _____

   b) Thinking about the long drive back home. _____

   c) The cat meowed. _____

   d) The street where I live. _____

   e) Some cows eating grass in the field. _____

   f) Walked slowly toward the door without looking at anyone. _____

   g) Hamid ran. _____

Combining Sentences

You can also use the joining words *or* and *so* to join two sentences.

Use *or* to join sentences when there are **two possibilities**, but **only one** will happen.

Example: He can walk to the library. He can ride his bike.
He can walk to the library, **or** *he can ride his bike.*

Use *so* when the idea in the second sentence happens **because of** the idea in the first sentence.

Example: There was deep snow on the ground. I wore my boots to school.
There was deep snow on the ground, **so** *I wore my boots to school.*

Remember to use a **comma before** the joining word.

1. Use *or* or *so* to join the two sentences.

a) I was tired. I went to bed.

_____

b) Kim might win the race. She might come in second.

_____

c) I can help you. You could ask Jeff for help.

_____

d) The sun was shining. I put on sunscreen.

_____

e) Is Travis coming? Is he still sick?

_____

f) The bus was coming. I ran to the bus stop.

_____

Correcting Run-On Sentences

A **run-on** sentence contains two complete ideas that are **not** correctly joined together. Look at the example below.

Example: I looked out the window I saw a bird.

Notice that "I looked out the window" is a complete idea, and "I saw a bird" is a complete idea. How could you correct this sentence?

You could use **a comma and a joining word** to join the ideas.

*Example: I looked out the window, **and** I saw a bird.*

You could **add a period** to make two separate sentences.

Example: I looked out the window. I saw a bird.

Remember that you **cannot** join two complete ideas with just a comma.

Example: I thought I had lost my keys, they were in my pocket.

To correct the sentence, you could **add a joining word** after the comma.

*Example: I thought I lost my keys, **but** they were in my pocket.*

You could **add a period** to make two separate sentences.

Example: I thought I lost my keys. They were in my pocket.

You **should not** join two complete ideas by using a joining word and no comma.

Example: Snow was falling so I put on my boots.

When you use a joining word to join two complete ideas, make sure you use a **comma before** the joining word.

*Example: Snow was falling, **so** I put on my boots.*

Always check your writing for run-on sentences. Correct any run-on sentences you find.

Remember that you can use a period to make two complete ideas into two separate sentences.

You can also use a comma **and** a joining word such as ***and***, ***but***, ***or***, or ***so*** to connect two complete ideas in a sentence.

Correcting Run-On Sentences

1. For each sentence below, write **RO** if it is a run-on sentence. Put a **check mark** if the sentence is correct.

   a) It is finally spring, and new leaves are growing on the trees. _____

   b) Cyrus caught a big fish, the one I caught was even bigger. _____

   c) The building was on fire and the fire trucks came quickly. _____

   d) The smoke detector wasn't working, so I replaced the battery. _____

   e) Sheila was going to play soccer with us but she hurt her foot. _____

   f) Ivan could take the dog for a walk or Karen might want to do it. _____

2. Show **two** ways to correct each **run-on sentence**. Look at the example.

   Example: We forgot to water the plants, they died.
   We forgot to water the plants. They died.
   We forgot to water the plants, so they died.

   a) I forgot my umbrella, I got wet in the rain.

   _____

   _____

   b) My foot slipped on the ice I didn't fall.

   _____

   _____

   c) I might get up early tomorrow, I might sleep in.

   _____

   _____

Common Nouns and Proper Nouns

A **noun** names a person, place, or thing.

A **common noun** names a person, place, or thing that is **not specific**.

A **proper noun** names a **specific** person, place, or thing. Proper nouns always start with **capital letters**. Look at the examples below.

Common Nouns (not specific)	Proper Nouns (specific)
month	February, October
city	Toronto, Calgary
person	Mr. Cantor, Julia, Aunt Phyllis

1. Add one **common noun** in each row. The common noun should fit the examples of proper nouns in the same row. The first row is completed for you.

Common Nouns	Examples of Proper Nouns
a) province	Ontario, Manitoba, Nova Scotia
b)	Saturn, Mars, Jupiter
c)	Elm Avenue, Riverside Drive
d)	Grenville Shoe Store, Bob's Electronics Shop
e)	Africa, South America, Asia
f)	Atlantic Ocean, Pacific Ocean
g)	Germany, China, India

2. Correct each sentence by making the **proper noun** start with a **capital letter**. Then underline the **common noun**.

a) The man took a train to regina on a rainy day.

b) Did wendy remember to buy jam at westside market?

c) My friend said that neptune is her favourite planet.

Exploring Proper Nouns

A **proper noun** names a **specific** person, place, or thing.
Proper nouns always start with **capital letters**.

Remember to use capital letters for the types of proper nouns shown below.

Note that the word **the** usually **does not** have a capital letter when it comes before a proper noun. *Example: We were amazed by the beauty of the Grand Canyon.*

Types of Proper Nouns	Examples of Proper Nouns
Names of **countries**, **provinces**, and **cities**	*Alberta, Saskatoon*
Names of **holidays**	*Labour Day, Valentine's Day*
Names of **people** and **pets**	*Jennifer, Dr. Silverman, Fluffy, Uncle George, Grandpa*
Names of **days of the week** and **months of the year**	*Thursday, November*
Names of **businesses**, **organizations**, and **museums**	*Free The Children, Royal Ontario Museum*
Names of **buildings**, **bridges**, and **monuments**	*Toronto City Hall, Confederation Bridge, National Artillery Monument*
Names of **languages**	*Spanish, German, Portuguese*
Names of **geographical places** and **features**	*Banff National Park, the Rocky Mountains*

1. Correct the sentences below by making the **proper nouns** start with **capital letters**.

a) Mr. chong drove across the peace bridge when he visited hamilton.

b) My grandparents will teach me to speak russian when they visit next january.

c) On mother's day, we visited the royal tyrell museum in alberta.

d) The rocky mountains stretch from canada to the united states.

e) Some people say english is more difficult to learn than french.

f) Tourists visiting ottawa often go to see the parliament buildings.

g) Students at lakeview school had a bake sale to help the united way raise money.

Spelling Plural Nouns

To make many nouns plural, just add the letter **s**.
Examples: lamp – lamps   gate – gates   paragraph – paragraphs

For nouns that end with **s, x, ch,** or **sh,** add **es**.
Examples: class – classes   fox – foxes   peach – peaches   wish – wishes

For nouns that end with a **consonant + y**, change the **y** to **i** and add **es**.
Examples: butterfly – butterflies   city – cities

For nouns that end with a **vowel + y**, just add **s**.
Examples: valley – valleys   chimney – chimneys

1. Write the **plural form** of each noun.

a) window _____

b) activity _____

c) lunch _____

d) brush _____

e) monkey _____

f) bus _____

g) tax _____

h) journey _____

i) eye _____

j) library _____

k) holiday _____

l) six _____

m) tray _____

n) beach _____

o) family _____

p) address _____

q) dish _____

r) virus _____

s) coach _____

t) island _____

u) berry _____

v) box _____

w) branch _____

x) eyelash _____

Spelling Plural Nouns

For some nouns that end with **o**, add **es**. For other nouns that end with **o**, just add **s**.

Add es

echo – echoes
hero – heroes
potato – potatoes
tomato – tomatoes

Just add s

patio – patios   video – videos
photo – photos   zero – zeros
piano – pianos
radio – radios

For most nouns that end with **f**, change the **f** to a **v** and add **es**. For a few nouns that end with **f**, just add the letter **s**.

Change f to v and add es

elf – elves   shelf – shelves
half – halves   thief – thieves
leaf – leaves   wolf – wolves
loaf – loaves

Just add s

chef – chefs   reef – reefs
chief – chiefs   roof – roofs
cliff – cliffs   sheriff – sheriffs

For some nouns that end with **fe**, change the **f** to a **v** and add **s**. For other nouns that end in **fe**, just add **s**.

Change f to v and add s   knife – knives   life – lives   wife – wives

Just add s   giraffe – giraffes   safe – safes

2. Complete each sentence by writing a **plural noun** shown above.

a) I often spend rainy days watching _____.

b) Biographies tell about the _____ of famous people.

c) We put _____ from our garden in the salad.

d) The store sells _____ and other musical instruments.

e) Police caught the _____ who stole the paintings.

f) A tornado blew the _____ off some houses.

g) The husbands and _____ dressed up for the fancy party.

h) Please pick up two _____ of bread at the grocery store.

Possessive Nouns

A **possessive noun** shows ownership.

Add an **apostrophe + s** to a **singular noun** to show ownership.

Most **plural nouns** end with **s**. Add an **apostrophe after the s** to show ownership.

Examples: The <u>car's</u> tires were flat. (One car has flat tires.)
The <u>cars'</u> tires were flat. (More than one car has flat tires.)

Add an **apostrophe + s** to a **plural noun** that **does not** end with **s**.

Example: We will collect the <u>people's</u> tickets as they enter the auditorium.

1. Rewrite each sentence. Use a **possessive noun** to replace the **underlined words** in each sentence. Check to see if the **underlined noun** is **singular** or **plural**.

a) We heard the shouts <u>of the children</u> from far away.

_____

b) The house <u>that belongs to my neighbours</u> is for sale.

_____

c) The paws <u>of the tiger</u> had very sharp claws.

_____

d) The chirping <u>of the birds</u> woke me up early.

_____

e) Will the teacher <u>of the students</u> give them homework?

_____

f) The laughter <u>of the women</u> echoed down the hallway.

_____

Action Verbs

The **subject** of a sentence is the person or thing that the sentence is about.

An **action verb** is a word that tells what the subject does or did. In the examples below, the subject is underlined and the action verb is in bold.

Example: <u>My sister</u> **swims** *in the lake.*
In this sentence, the verb *swims* tells what the subject (*my sister*) does.

Example: <u>A large branch</u> **fell** *onto our driveway.*
In this sentence, the verb *fell* tells what the subject (*a large branch*) did.

The verbs *swims* and *fell* both express action, so these verbs are action verbs.

1. Underline the **action verbs** in the sentences below. **Do not** underline a verb that **does not** express an action.

a) Fireworks exploded in the night sky.

b) The teacher asked us questions about the story.

c) Ali is always tired after hockey practice.

d) The wind blew leaves off the trees.

e) Shawna tripped on her way up the stairs.

f) The car drove right through a red light.

g) My uncle is a police officer.

h) The flag flaps high above our heads.

i) Mr. Phong gave us each an apple.

j) Mom told me about her tough day at work.

k) The sun shines brightly on clear days.

l) The children were happy all day long.

Linking Verbs

A **linking verb** is a verb that does **not** show an action.

Look at the verbs in the sentences below. Notice that these verbs do **not** show an **action** that someone did or is doing.

Examples: *The spaghetti **was** tasty.*
*Orlando **seems** tired today.*
*Mrs. Gupta **is** a veterinarian.*

The verbs in the sentences above are all linking verbs.

What does a linking verb do if it doesn't show action?

1. A linking verb can link the **subject** of the sentence (the person or thing the sentence is about) to an adjective that describes the subject.

*Example: The spaghetti **was** tasty.*

The subject of the sentence is the noun *spaghetti*. The adjective *tasty* describes the subject. The linking verb *was* links the subject to the adjective that describes it.

*Example: Orlando **seems** tired today.*

The subject of the sentence is the proper noun *Orlando*. The adjective *tired* describes the subject. The linking verb *seems* links the subject to the adjective that describes it.

2. A linking verb can link the **subject** of the sentence to a noun that is another name for the subject.

*Example: Mrs. Gupta **is** a veterinarian.*

The subject of the sentence is the proper noun *Mrs. Gupta*. The noun *veterinarian* is another name for the subject. The linking verb *is* links the subject to a noun that is another name for the subject. So *Mrs. Gupta* and *veterinarian* are two nouns that name the same person.

Linking Verbs

1. The **subject** in each sentence is underlined. The **linking verb** is in bold. Circle the **adjective** that describes the subject **or** the **noun** that is another name for the subject. Then circle the **correct answer** in the next sentence.

   a) <u>Leo</u> **was** excited about the party.
   The linking verb connects the subject to (an adjective   a noun).

   b) My <u>sister</u> **seemed** upset about something.
   The linking verb connects the subject to (an adjective   a noun).

   c) His <u>uncle</u> **is** a nurse at the hospital.
   The linking verb connects the subject to (an adjective   a noun).

   d) The <u>students</u> **became** restless right before recess.
   The linking verb connects the subject to (an adjective   a noun).

   e) My <u>grandmother</u> **was** a dancer many years ago.
   The linking verb connects the subject to (an adjective   a noun).

2. Underline the **linking verb** in each sentence.

   a) The thunderstorm sounds very close now.

   b) This ice cream tastes minty.

   c) Our attic is home to many mice.

   d) The leftover chicken bones become stock for chicken soup.

   e) John seems nervous about meeting his new neighbours.

   f) My friend Nami became a great piano player.

   g) An earthworm's body feels slimy.

   h) The flowers in Mom's garden smell wonderful.

Spelling Past Tense Verbs

For many verbs, just add **ed** to make the past tense.

Examples: **Present tense**: *Yuki and Ella <u>jump</u> into the swimming pool.*
Past tense: *Yuki and Ella <u>jumped</u> into the swimming pool.*
Past tense with has: *Yuki has <u>jumped</u> into the swimming pool.*
Past tense with have: *Yuki and Ella have <u>jumped</u> into the swimming pool.*

If the verb ends with **e**, just add **d**.

Examples: **Present tense**: *I <u>tie</u> my shoelaces.*
Past tense: *I <u>tied</u> my shoelaces.*
Present tense: *I <u>fill</u> the glass with milk.*
Past tense: *I <u>filled</u> the glass with milk.*

If the verb ends with a **consonant + y**, change the **y** to **i** and add **ed**.

Examples: **Present tense**: *Luca and Ken <u>carry</u> the books upstairs.*
Past tense: *Luca and Ken have <u>carried</u> the books upstairs.*

If a **one-syllable** verb ends with a **consonant + vowel + consonant**, and the final consonant is **not w, x,** or **y**, double the final consonant and add **ed**.

Examples: **Present tense**: *The cars <u>stop</u> at the red light.*
Past tense: *The cars <u>stopped</u> at the red light.*
Present tense: *See the horse <u>trot</u> around the ring.*
Past tense: *The horse <u>trotted</u> around the ring.*

Do not double the final consonant for a verb that ends with **one vowel + w, x,** or **y**.

Examples: **Present tense**: *The girls <u>row</u> the boat to the shore.*
Past tense: *The girls <u>rowed</u> the boat to the shore.*
Present tense: *The protests <u>delay</u> the construction of the dam.*
Past tense: *The protests <u>delayed</u> the construction of the dam.*

Do not double the final consonant of a verb that **ends with two consonants**.

Examples: **Present tense**: *The candles <u>burn</u> brightly this evening.*
Past tense: *The candles <u>burned</u> brightly this evening.*
Present tense: *I <u>lift</u> the garbage pail.*
Past tense: *I <u>lifted</u> the garbage pail.*

Spelling Past Tense Verbs

> **Do not** double the final consonant of a verb that ends with **two vowels and a consonant.**
>
> *Examples:* **Present tense:** *The students* <u>complain</u> *about too much homework.*
> **Past tense:** *The students* <u>complain**ed**</u> *about too much homework.*
> **Present tense:** *The scientists* <u>look</u> *into the microscope.*
> **Past tense:** *The scientists* <u>look**ed**</u> *into the microscope.*

1. Write and correctly spell the **past tense** of the verb in brackets.

a) The runner _____ in two races. (compete)

b) I _____ my foot as I listened to the music. (tap)

c) The squirrel _____ up the oak tree. (climb)

d) Mr. Sanchez _____ the guests as they arrived. (greet)

e) Marco has _____ hard for the science test. (study)

f) On her last visit, my aunt _____ with us for ten days. (stay)

g) Have the workers _____ the leaky roof yet? (fix)

h) I _____ the shopping list to the bulletin board. (pin)

i) The teacher has _____ the writing on the chalkboard. (erase)

j) John _____ up for a book on the bookshelf. (reach)

k) Keisha _____ for half an hour every day last week. (jog)

l) I _____ the children to stay away from the train tracks. (warn)

Past Tense of Irregular Verbs

An **irregular verb** does not follow the rules that apply to other verbs. Make sure you use the correct **past tense** of the irregular verbs on this page.

For the verbs in the chart below, notice that the past tense is **the same,** whether or not the helping verb *has* or *have* is used.

Verb	Present Tense	Past Tense with or Without *Has* or *Have*
to bend	bend, bends	bent
to build	build, builds	built
to buy	buy, buys	bought
to catch	catch, catches	caught
to cut	cut, cuts	cut
to feed	feed, feeds	fed
to find	find, finds	found
to sleep	sleep, sleeps	slept
to understand	understand, understands	understood
to spend	spend, spends	spent

For the verbs in the next chart, notice that **a different form** of the past tense is used with the helping verbs **has** or **have**.

Verb	Present Tense	Past Tense	Past Tense with *Has* or *Have*
to be	am, are, is	was, were	been
to begin	begin, begins	began	begun
to bite	bite, bites	bit	bitten
to break	break, breaks	broke	broken
to come	come, comes	came	come
to drink	drink, drinks	drank	drunk
to drive	drive, drives	drove	driven
to eat	eat, eats	ate	eaten
to hide	hide, hides	hid	hidden
to give	give, gives	gave	given

Past Tense of Irregular Verbs

1. Write the correct **past tense** of the verb in brackets.

a) The children have _____ all the orange juice. (drink)

b) Liam has _____ his dog to baseball practice. (bring)

c) I _____ through most of the boring movie. (sleep)

d) We wondered if Dad has _____ Mom the gift yet. (give)

e) She _____ to hum softly to herself. (begin)

f) Mosquitoes have _____ nearly all of the hikers. (bite)

g) My grandmother has _____ three fish so far today. (catch)

h) Winter weather has _____ once again. (come)

i) My little brother _____ a castle with his toy blocks. (build)

j) I have _____ the treasure map in a safe place. (hide)

k) He spoke very quickly, but I _____ what he said. (understand)

l) Carlos walked the dog and _____ the cat. (feed)

m) We have _____ looking for you all afternoon! (be)

n) Lou and I will go for a bike ride after we have _____ dinner. (eat)

o) Mrs. Polanski _____ over to pick up the crying child. (bend)

p) We have _____ down this road many times before. (drive)

q) The thief _____ the stolen jewels. (hide)

r) Earlier this morning, Dad _____ the grass in the backyard. (cut)

s) My parents have _____ your parents for a long time. (know)

Using *Should* and *Could*

Should and *could* are **helping verbs**.

Use *should* when someone is giving **advice** or a **suggestion**.
Example: You <u>should</u> go to bed early if you are very tired.

Use *should* for an action that someone **expects** will happen.
Example: It is a warm day, so the snow <u>should</u> melt quickly.

Use *could* for actions that someone was **able to do in the past**.
Example: When Mr. Thomas was younger, he <u>could</u> jog five kilometres.

Use *could* when <u>talking</u> about a **possibility** or **something that might be true**.
Examples: After school, we <u>could</u> watch a video at my house. (possibility)
Mrs. Rossi <u>could</u> be at work right now. (might be true)

1. Complete each sentence with **_should_** or **_could_**. Under the sentence, underline the **reason for your answer**.

a) When she was younger, she _____ swim across the bay.
   (advice/suggestion, expected action, ability in the past, possibility/might be true)

b) Paul is never late, so he _____ arrive on time today.
   (advice/suggestion, expected action, ability in the past, possibility or might be true)

c) Mom said I _____ look for my scarf on the floor of the closet.
   (advice/suggestion, expected action, ability in the past, possibility or might be true)

d) If your nose is running, you _____ have a cold.
   (advice/suggestion, expected action, ability in the past, possibility or might be true)

e) The volcano hasn't erupted in years, but it _____ erupt again.
   (advice/suggestion, expected action, ability in the past, possibility or might be true)

f) I turned on the heater, so the room _____ warm up soon.
   (advice/suggestion, expected action, ability in the past, possibility or might be true)

g) You _____ always tell the truth if you want people to trust you.
   (advice/suggestion, expected action, ability in the past, possibility or might be true)

Using the Correct Verb Tense

Use **present tense** verbs for actions that happen in the **present**.

Examples: I <u>tell</u> my cousins all about my trip to Utah.
I <u>am telling</u> my cousins all about my trip to Utah.

Use **past tense** verbs for actions that happened in the **past**.

Examples: I <u>told</u> my cousins all about my trip to Utah.
I <u>have told</u> my cousins all about my trip to Utah.
I <u>was telling</u> my cousins all about my trip to Utah when you called.

Use **future tense** verbs for actions that will happen in the **future**.

Example: I <u>will tell</u> my cousins all about my trip to Utah.

1. In each sentence, write the **correct tense** of the verb in brackets. Look for clues that tell you whether the action happens in the present, past, or future.

a) I _____ the dog on a long walk tomorrow. (take)

b) Last week, Leah _____ her ankle while jogging. (sprain)

c) I can't come right now because I _____ a bath. (take)

d) She _____ to school when it suddenly started to rain. (walk)

e) Now I _____ why my brother is angry with me. (understand)

f) Soon these shoes _____ too small for me. (are)

g) The choir _____ two songs at the concert last night. (sing)

h) Dad _____ the grass when the lawnmower broke. (cut)

i) It _____, and I am getting very wet! (rains)

j) I stare at the sky and _____ the clouds go by. (watch)

k) Julio _____ catch with you after he eats his lunch. (play)

l) My cousin's dog _____ with us all next week. (stay)

Pronouns and Antecedents

A **pronoun** is a word that takes the place of a **noun**.

Use the pronouns below to take the place of nouns that name **people**:
I you he she we they me him her us them

Use the pronouns below to take the place of nouns that name **things**:

it they them

1. Complete each sentence with the correct **pronoun**. The pronoun takes the place of the word or words in brackets.

   a) _____ has become an amazing baseball player. (Angela)

   b) I was sure I had put _____ in my coat pocket. (the keys)

   c) We hope Claire and Anthony can come with _____. (you and me)

   d) _____ will work together on the science project. (Yuki and I)

   e) Are _____ going to come to the concert? (your parents)

   f) My name is Fred. _____ will be your guide on the tour. (Fred)

2. Use a **pronoun** to replace the word or words in brackets below the blank.

   a) I gave _____ to _____ to buy milk at school.
                (money)   (Lynn and Jo)

   b) _____ is coming to meet _____ tomorrow.
      (Mike)   (my cousins)

   c) If you have questions, ask _____ or _____.
                    (Josh)   (Amy)

   d) I will give the books to _____ if _____ have not read
            (my sisters)   (Tina and Lily)

   _____ already.
   (the books)

Adjectives Before and After Nouns

An **adjective** is a word that describes a noun. An adjective can come **before** or **after** the noun it describes. In both examples below, the adjective *beautiful* describes the noun *sunset*.

Before a noun: *We looked at the (beautiful) sunset.*

After a noun: *The sunset was (beautiful)*

1. Circle the **adjective** in each sentence. Underline the **noun** the adjective describes. Draw an arrow from the adjective to the **noun it describes**.

a) I think I'll wear the striped sweater today.

b) Give me the clothes that are dirty, and I'll wash them.

c) If the movie is long, I won't watch it before going to bed.

d) The man who found the expensive necklace returned it to the owner.

e) The woman was brave to chase after the thief as he ran away.

2. Circle the **noun** and underline the **adjective** that describes it.

a) Our dog was so fluffy after her bath!

b) It's so exciting to find a surprise package in the mailbox!

c) The pants looked the right size, but the legs were too long.

d) In summer, we sometimes get severe thunderstorms.

e) They say that every cloud has a silver lining.

f) Jack waded through the slippery mud to cross the shallow stream.

g) The gowns the women wore were glamorous.

h) Alice is nervous about speaking in front of an audience.

Adjectives Before and After Nouns

3. Look for **more than one** adjective in each sentence. Circle each **adjective**, and underline each **noun**.

   a) Fierce warriors surrounded the ancient castle.

   b) Dad thought the old movie we watched was hilarious.

   c) Don't walk over the shiny floor in your muddy boots!

   d) Max was curious about the new restaurant, so he went there for lunch.

   e) A huge spider crawled slowly down the wall beside my bed.

   f) After the long hike, my legs were sore and stiff.

   g) Red and white balloons decorated the huge auditorium.

4. Look at the list of adjectives below. Read the sentence first. Then write the **adjective** that **fits best**.

   silver thirsty peaceful morning hungry frightened summer bravest

   a) On a sunny _____ day, my family goes to the park for a picnic.

   b) Tiny _____ minnows swim by the shoreline.

   c) Even the _____ men were terrified of the bear.

   d) No amount of coaxing could make the tiny _____ kitten climb down the tree.

   e) The boy was warned not to bother the _____ cat while it was sleeping.

   f) The warm _____ sunshine poured into her bedroom.

   g) The hikers were _____ and _____after climbing the mountainside.

Adjectives Can Describe How Many

An **adjective** describes a noun. Some adjectives answer the question "How many?" **Numbers** can be adjectives.

Example: Ted has (three) cats.
Three is an adjective that describes the noun **cats**.

Some adjectives answer the question "How many?" but they **do not** describe exactly how many.

Example: I have (some) pens.
Some is an adjective that describes the noun **pens**.

1. Circle each **adjective** that answers the question "**How many?**" Underline the **noun** the adjective describes.

a) The teacher wrote several questions on the board.

b) At the end of art class, each student handed in sketches.

c) We put up posters for the play, but few people came.

d) I used both hands to cover my eyes.

e) My two brothers helped me shovel the driveway.

f) Did you know that all snakes are reptiles?

g) Most people recycle newspapers and cans.

h) Hundreds of fans showed up for the concert.

i) Many children wanted to pat the dog and he got scared.

j) Ten bundles of newspapers are delivered here every morning.

Demonstrative Adjectives

A demonstrative adjective answers the questions, "Which one?" or "Which ones?"
The words **this**, **that**, **these**, and **those** are demonstrative adjectives.

Use **this** and **that** with singular nouns. Use **these** and **those** with plural nouns. Use **this** and **these** for people or things that are close. Use **that** and **those** for people and things that are farther away.

In the examples below, the demonstrative adjective is in bold, and the noun it describes is underlined.

*The blue shirt is nice, but I like **that** shirt better.*
*Ricardo, please put **these** books back on the shelf.*
***This** movie is better than the movie we watched yesterday.*
*I wonder if **those** gloves on the table are mine.*

1. Rewrite the sentence, using the correct form of the **demonstrative adjective**.

   a) These people over by the tree are my friends.

   _____

   b) Will one of those keys in my hand open the lock?

   _____

   c) That box I'm carrying is very heavy.

   _____

   d) Please leave through this door at the end of the hall.

   _____

   e) Those socks I'm wearing are very warm.

   _____

   f) This rainbow in the sky is beautiful.

   _____

Using Adjectives to Compare

You can use **adjectives** to **compare** two or more things.

Example: A lion is <u>faster</u> than a horse, but a cheetah is the fastest mammal.

The adjective **faster** compares two mammals. The adjective **fastest** compares all mammals.

Follow the rules below to create **adjectives that compare**.

1. Add **er** to many adjectives to compare **two things**.
Example: bright – brighter   A lamp is <u>brighter</u> than a candle.

2. Add **est** to many adjectives to compare **more than two things**. Use **the** before the
adjective.
Example: tall – tallest   Kate is the <u>tallest</u> person on my swim team.

3. For adjectives that end with **e**, just add **r** or **st**.
Example: large – larger – largest

4. For adjectives that end with a **consonant + y**, change the **y** to an **i** and add **er**
or **est**.
Example: funny – funnier – funniest

5. For adjectives that end with a **single vowel + consonant**, double the final
consonant and add **er** or **est**.
Example: big – bigger – biggest

1. Change the **adjective** in brackets to make it compare **two things** or **more than
two things**. Remember to write **the** before an adjective that ends with **est**.

a) The green shirt is _____ than the blue shirt. (nice)

b) This apartment building is _____ building on the street. (tall)

c) My new quilt is _____ than the one I had before. (pretty)

d) Tuesday was _____ than Thursday, but Wednesday was

_____ day last week. (hot)

Using Adjectives to Compare

Make sure you use the correct form of these **adjectives that compare**.

Adjective	To Compare Two Things	To Compare More Than Two Things
good	better	best
bad	worse	worst
far	farther	farthest
many or some	more	most

2. Use the correct form of the **adjective** in brackets. Write *the* before an adjective that compares **more than two things**.

a) The soup he made yesterday was _____ than the soup he made last week. (good)

b) Darnell is _____ batter of all the players on our baseball team. (good)

c) Gina's house is _____ from the library than your house is. (far)

d) The sequel to the movie was _____ than the original movie. (bad)

e) All the malls in our city have lots of stores, but Crestview Mall has

_____ stores. (many)

f) Go past these doors, and you will see that the washroom is _____ door at the end of the hall. (far)

g) Laurie found many seashells, but Jeremy found _____ than she did. (many)

h) This is _____ snowstorm we've had in many years. (bad)

i) I am working harder this year, so I am getting _____ marks than I did last year. (good)

Adverbs Can Describe How

An **adverb** describes a **verb**. Some adverbs describe **how** an action happens. Look at the examples below.

Lionel politely asked for directions.
The adverb **politely** describes **how** Lionel asked.

The two drivers shouted angrily at each other.
The adverb **angrily** describes **how** the drivers shouted.

Not all adverbs end with **ly**. **Well** can be an adverb, but it does not end with **ly**.

Example: He played the piano well at the recital.

Don't be fooled by **adjectives** that end with **ly**.

Example: The cat ran away with the smelly sock.

1. Circle the **adverbs** that tell how an action happens. Underline the **verb** that each adverb describes. Draw an arrow from each adverb **to the verb it describes**.

   a) The children spoke quietly while their father slept peacefully.

   b) He gently laid the baby in the crib, and then he silently left the room.

   c) I clumsily dropped a dish, which shattered noisily against the floor.

   d) The volcano erupted violently and unexpectedly.

2. Decide whether the underlined adverb describes **how** the action happened. Circle **Yes** or **No**.

   a) We walked to school <u>quickly</u> in the chilly weather.   **Yes   No**

   b) The lonely man had a lovely garden, which he watered <u>daily</u>.   **Yes   No**

   c) Silly Miranda likes fast cars, and she likes to drive <u>fast</u>, too.   **Yes   No**

   d) The lively party ended <u>suddenly</u> when he <u>rudely</u> told everyone to leave.   **Yes No**

Adverbs Can Describe When or How Often

An **adverb** describes a **verb**. Some adverbs describe **when** an action happens.

Example: Carlos swam with us today
The adverb **today** describes **when** Carlos swam.

Some adverbs describe **how often** an action happens.

Example: Mrs. Grant jogs frequently
The adverb **frequently** describes **how often** Mrs. Grant jogs.

1. Circle whether the **underlined** adverb tells **when** or **how often** an action happens.

a) Let's meet <u>later</u> to discuss our plans.   **when   how often**

b) Ingrid <u>sometimes</u> forgets to bring her homework.   **when   how often**

c) We drive to Buffalo <u>occasionally</u>.   **when   how often**

d) Have we met <u>before</u>?   **when   how often**

e) My whole family is going to watch a movie <u>tonight</u>.   **when   how often**

f) She checked the clock <u>constantly</u> while waiting for her date.   **when   how often**

g) Hal had long hair <u>a year ago</u>, but he cut it short <u>last week</u>.   **when   how often**

h) People <u>rarely ever</u> find bits of gold just lying in a creek bed.   **when   how often**

i) The judge will make her decision <u>tomorrow</u>.   **when   how often**

j) We <u>never</u> see bears in these woods.   **when   how often**

k) Tony cleans his room <u>regularly</u>.   **when   how often**

l) <u>Sometimes</u> she forgets, but <u>usually</u> she remembers.   **when   how often**

m) I <u>seldom</u> see Margaret, but I talk to her brother <u>often</u>.   **when   how often**

Adverbs Can Describe Where

An **adverb** describes a **verb**. Some adverbs describe **where** an action happens.
Example: The children played outside.
The adverb **outside** describes **where** the children played.

Some adverbs describe **where** an action happens, but they **do not** describe **exactly where** it happens.
Examples: anywhere   nowhere

Some adverbs describe a **direction** rather than where an action happens.
Example: When she let go of the balloon, it drifted upward.

The adverb **upward** describes the **direction** in which the balloon drifted.

1. Circle the **adverb** that tells **where** an action happens.

   a) Please sit here during the performance.

   b) We were searching for a mailbox, and we found one nearby.

   c) The grey cat followed us everywhere.

   d) Devin watches old movies downstairs.

   e) A mouse lives somewhere in our house.

2. Circle each adverb that tells the **direction** an action happens.

   a) I wonder if ants can walk backward.

   b) This bus travels south on Poplar Road.

   c) The road was blocked, so we could not move forward.

   d) The crowd looked up at the helicopter.

   e) My little sister ran to the left to hide. When I looked for her, she ran to the right.

Exploring Adverbs That Compare

An **adverb** describes a **verb**. Some adverbs **compare** how actions are done. With some short adverbs, you can add **er** to compare **two** actions, and **est** to compare **more than two** actions.

Example: Judy ran fast. Kai ran faster than Judy. Melissa ran the fastest.

In each sentence above, the circled adverb describes the verb **ran**.
The adverb **faster** compares **two** actions—how Kai ran and how Judy ran.
The adverb **fastest** compares **more than two** actions—how Judy ran, how Kai ran, and how Melissa ran. Melissa ran the fastest of all three people.

You can use the endings **er** and **est** with the adverb **early**. Change the **y** to an **i** and add **er** or **est**.

Example: early – earlier – earliest

1. Complete each sentence by adding **er** or **est** to the adverb in brackets. Think about how many actions are being compared in each sentence. Remember to write **the** before an adverb that compares **more than two** actions.

a) My brother, my sister, and I can all jump high, but my brother jumps

_____. (high)

b) My little sister walks _____ than I walk. (slow)

c) The sun shines _____ than the moon. (bright)

d) Sally sang _____ of all the people in the choir. (loud)

e) Many people ran in the race, but I ran _____. (slow)

f) Michael did his homework _____ than Rosa did hers. (fast)

g) I am taller than Joe, so I can reach _____ than he can. (high)

h) Mrs. Cortez gets up _____ than Mr. Cortez. (early)

i) All four people in my family get up early, but I get up _____.(early)

Adverbs Can Describe Verbs, Adjectives, and Adverbs

An **adverb** can describe a **verb**. An **adverb** can also describe an **adjective**. Adverbs that describe **adjectives** often answer the question "How?"

Example: My little brother is <u>very</u> shy.

Shy is an adjective that describes the noun **brother**. **Very** is an **adverb** that describes the adjective **shy**. **Very** answers the question "How shy?"

Example: An <u>extremely</u> valuable painting was stolen from the art gallery.

Valuable is an adjective that describes the noun **painting**. **Extremely** is an **adverb** that describes the adjective **valuable**. **Extremely** answers the question "How valuable?"

An **adverb** can also describe another **adverb**.

Example: Shawn walked <u>quite</u> quickly, so he wouldn't be late for school.

Quickly is an adverb that describes the verb **walked**. **Quite** is an adverb that describes the adverb **quickly**. Adverbs that describe other adverbs often answer the question "How?" **Quite** answers the question "How quickly?"

1. Circle each **adverb** that describes an **adjective**. Draw an arrow to the **adjective that the adverb describes**.

a) Dad was slightly annoyed that I had not cleaned my room.

b) The roof of our house was badly damaged during the hurricane.

c) The Hoover Dam is an incredibly huge structure.

d) Maggie was quite interested in hearing about my trip to Africa.

e) I thanked the librarian for being so helpful to me.

f) We didn't swim in the lake because the water was awfully cold.

g) The children couldn't sleep because they had watched a really scary movie.

Punctuating Dialogue

Use **quotation marks** around words that someone is speaking.

Examples: "The laundry should be dry by now," <u>*Dad said*</u>*.*
"I lived in Ireland before I moved here," <u>*explained Rachel*</u>*.*
"We're over here," <u>*called Katie*</u>*.*

The underlined words are called **speaker tags**. A speaker tag tells who is talking. When the speaker tag comes **after** the spoken words, remember to put a comma **before** the **second** quotation mark. See the examples above.

When the speaker tag comes **after** the spoken words, **do not** put a **comma** before the second quotation mark if there is a **question mark** or **exclamation point** at the end of the spoken words.

Examples: "Can we go to the mall tomorrow?" asked Gary.
"I'm so happy to see you!" exclaimed Aunt Mary.

If the speaker tag comes **before** the spoken words, put a comma **after** the speaker tag.

Example: The salesperson said, "Jeans are on sale this week."

Remember to use a **capital letter** for the first spoken word.

1. Add **quotation marks** to each sentence below. Add a **comma**, if necessary.

a) We've won the game!   shouted Chris.

b) I hope we have good weather during our vacation   Dad said.

c) I wonder if she noticed that we came in late   whispered Beth.

d) Would you like to look through the telescope?   the scientist asked.

e) The coach said   Now that's what I call teamwork!

f) The crowd shouted   Don't go yet! Sing one more song!

g) My mom said   I think I've seen this movie before.

h) This produce is all organically grown the woman explained.

Punctuating Dialogue

In your writing, if someone says a long sentence, you can put the speaker tag **in the middle** of the sentence. Look at the example below.

"I know I put my watch in a safe place," *said Rick,* *"but I can't remember where."*

If you are putting the speaker tag in the middle of a long spoken sentence, remember to do the following:

- Put **quotation marks** around the **first part** of the spoken sentence **and** the **second part** of the spoken sentence.

- Put a **comma** at the end of the **first part** of the spoken sentence, **before** the second quotation mark.

- Put a **comma** after the **speaker tag**.

- Put a **period**, **question mark**, or **exclamation mark** at the end of the **second part** of the spoken sentence, **before** the last quotation mark.

- Remember that you **do not** need a **capital letter** on the first word of the **second part** of the spoken sentence, since all the spoken words make up one sentence.

2. Add the **correct punctuation** to the sentences below.

a) My baby cried most of the night   said Mrs. Hernandez   and I think it was because she had a fever

b) The woman who lives next door is a doctor   explained Mr. Carson   but she retired several years ago

c) These red roses are pretty   said the gardener   and the pink roses are even prettier

d) It has been snowing all morning   said Rita   so I think I'll need to wear my boots when I go outside this afternoon

e) My parents said you could come to the amusement park with us   said Eddie but will you be able to get to my house by noon

Write the Correct Word

Don't be confused by the words below. Check your writing to make sure you have written the right words.

Word	Definition and Example
all ready	completely prepared *Example: I had packed my suitcase, and I was **all ready** for the trip.*
already	before now or before a specific time *Example: I have **already** finished my homework.*
desert	a dry area of land, often covered with sand *Example: The explorer walked across the hot **desert**.*
dessert	sweet food eaten at the end of a meal *Example: We ate spaghetti, and then we had ice cream for **dessert**.*
it's	the contraction for the words **it is** or **it has** *Examples: **It's** time to go now. **It's** been sunny all week.*
its	a possessive pronoun that means **belonging to it** *Example: The squirrel sat up on **its** hind legs.*

1. In the sentence, circle the **correct choice** in the brackets.

   a) The airplane made an emergency landing in the (desert   dessert).

   b) Swimming is fun, and (it's   its) a great way to get exercise.

   c) I called her house, but she had (all ready   already) left for school.

   d) My favourite (desert   dessert) is chocolate pudding.

   e) I had studied my notes carefully, so I was (all ready   already) for the test.

   f) The bus might be late because (it's   its) been snowing all morning.

   g) Have you (all ready   already) seen this movie?

   h) The wagon was missing one of (it's   its) wheels.

Student Writing Tips

Sentence Starters

Sentence starters for **stating your opinion** in a piece of writing:

In my opinion...	I think...	The best thing about...
I feel...	I prefer...	The worst thing about...
I believe...	I know...	_____ is better than _____

Sentence starters to use **when trying to persuade someone** in a piece of writing:

Of course...	Clearly...	The fact is...
Without doubt...	Everyone knows that...	It is clear that...

Transition Words

Transition words or phrases to use **when providing reasons** in a piece of writing:

First of all...	Next...	Most importantly...
Secondly...	Another reason...	To begin with...

Transition words or phrases to use **when providing examples** in a piece of writing:

For example...	In fact...	In addition...
For instance...	In particular...	Another example...

Transition words or phrases to **show cause and effect** in a piece of writing:

For this reason...	As a result...	Consequently...
Because of [fact]...	Therefore...	Due to [reason]...

Transition words to use **when comparing or contrasting** in a piece of writing:

Similarly...	But...	Although...
Like...	However...	Even though...

Transition words or phrases to use **when showing a sequence** in a piece of writing:

First...	Next...	After that...
Second...	Eventually...	Lastly...

Transition words or phrases to use **when concluding** a piece of writing:

Finally...	Lastly...	All in all...
In conclusion...	To sum up...	As you can see...

Editing Checklist

Capitalization

☐ I used capital letters correctly in the title.

☐ I used capital letters for the first word in each sentence.

☐ I used capital letters for all proper nouns.

Organization

☐ I checked for run-on sentences.

☐ I have included a variety of sentence types and lengths.

☐ I organized and grouped related information together.

☐ I used headings and other formatting when needed.

☐ I used powerful verbs and interesting adjectives.

Punctuation

☐ I used the correct punctuation mark at the end of every sentence. (. ! ?)

☐ I used commas correctly in sentences.

☐ I used apostrophes correctly in contractions and possessives.

☐ I used quotation marks correctly to punctuate dialogue.

Spelling and Sentence Structure

☐ All my sentences are complete sentences.

☐ I used appropriate verb tenses (past, present, future).

☐ I checked for subject-verb agreement (singular verbs with singular subjects; plural verbs with plural subjects).

☐ I checked and corrected spelling as necessary.

Think
A.R.M.S

Think
C.O.P.S

Add

• Did I add words/sentences?

Remove

• Did I remove unneeded words/sentences that don't make sense?

Move

• Did move words or sentences into a better order to make more sense?

Substitute

• Did I substitute boring or overused words for stronger more interesting words?

Capitalization

• Do my sentences and proper nouns have capital letters?

Organization

• Did I order my ideas in a way that makes sense?

Punctuation

• Do my sentences have end marks? (.!?)

Spelling

• Did I check my spelling to the best of my ability?

MY RESTAURANT: _____

Restaurant Description

_____

_____

_____

_____

Design a restaurant menu! First, choose foods for your menu. Then, write a detailed description for each menu item. Use interesting words to make customers' mouths water!

Starters

_____

_____

_____

_____

Main Courses

_____

_____

_____

_____

Dessert Specials

_____

_____

_____

☐ My writing makes sense.

☐ My descriptions will make people want to order the food.

☐ I checked for correct spelling and punctuation.

> Create a logo for your restaurant. Design and publish your menu.

Describe Your Dream Home

Design and describe your dream home. Add details about the exterior and interior. On a separate page, draw your dream home.

My dream home would be...

_____

_____

_____

_____

_____

_____

_____

_____

_____

_____

_____

_____

_____

_____

_____

☐ My writing makes sense.   ☐ I used descriptive words and phrases.

☐ My picture is neat and colourful.   ☐ I checked for correct spelling and punctuation.

Expository Writing Checklist

 Learning Goal

I can explain, describe, give information, or inform a reader about a topic.

 Success Criteria

Introduction

- ☐ I will think about the purpose and target audience for my writing.
- ☐ I will have an attention-grabbing opening sentence that hooks the reader.
- ☐ I will clearly introduce the topic of my writing.

Idea Development

- ☐ I will include ____ paragraphs or sections about my topic.
- ☐ I will answer the reader's basic questions about the topic such as: Who? What? Where? When? Why? How?
- ☐ I will develop the topic using facts, examples, explanations, and details.
- ☐ I will use topic-specific vocabulary to help explain the topic.
- ☐ I will write a strong conclusion that supports my point of view.

Organization

- ☐ I will organize and group related information together, and use headings and other formatting.
- ☐ I will use transition words and phrases to connect my ideas.

Sentence Structure, Grammar, and Word Usage

- ☐ I will use a variety of sentence types.
- ☐ I will use topic-related vocabulary.
- ☐ I will check for correct grammar and spelling.

My Non-Fiction Report

Topic: _____

_____

_____

_____

_____

_____

_____

_____

_____

_____

_____

_____

_____

_____

_____

_____

_____

_____

☐ I checked for correct spelling.　　☐ I organized my ideas in a way that makes sense.

☐ I checked for correct punctuation.　☐ I used linking words to connect my ideas.

Exploring Persuasive Writing

Persuasive writing gives your opinion and tries to convince the reader to agree with you.

Read the statement below. Write a persuasive paragraph to convince the reader of your opinion. Make sure to add details to support your thinking.

"Kids should have their own mobile phones."

I (agree, disagree) that kids should have their own mobile phones.

_____

_____

_____

_____

_____

_____

_____

_____

_____

_____

_____

_____

☐ I checked for correct spelling.   ☐ I organized my ideas in a way that makes sense.

☐ I checked for correct punctuation.   ☐ I used linking words to connect my ideas.

☐ I used interesting words.   ☐ I used a figure of speech.

Book "Sales Pitch"

Title: _____

Author: _____

Genre: _____

Author's purpose: ☐ to inform   ☐ to entertain   ☐ to persuade

Pretend you are an author with a book for sale.
Write a persuasive "sales pitch" to convince consumers to buy your book.
A "sales pitch" is a speech that persuades someone to buy something.

Book summary:

_____

_____

_____

_____

Sales pitch:

_____

_____

_____

_____

_____

_____

☐ I checked for correct spelling.   ☐ I organized my ideas in a way that makes sense.

☐ I checked for correct punctuation.   ☐ I used linking words to connect my ideas.

☐ I used interesting words.   ☐ I used a figure of speech.

What Is Your Opinion?

An **opinion** is a belief or feeling about a topic.

Opinion sentence starters:

- I prefer...
- I believe...
- I think...
- I feel...
- The best thing about...
- The worst part about...
- Everyone should...
- I agree/disagree with...

State your opinion: _____

_____

First of all, _____

_____

_____

_____

Another reason _____

_____

_____

_____

Also, _____

_____

_____

_____

This is why _____

☐ I checked for correct spelling.   ☐ I organized my ideas in a way that makes sense.

☐ I checked for correct punctuation.   ☐ I used linking words to connect my ideas.

Exploring Idioms

Idioms are common expressions that are understood by people and that mean something different than their literal meaning.

1. Use each idiom in a sentence to show its correct meaning.

   a) hit the books

   _____

   b) hit the nail on the head

   _____

   c) when pigs fly

   _____

   d) stir up a hornets nest

   _____

   e) cool as a cucumber

   _____

   f) in hot water

   _____

   g) in the same boat

   _____

   h) add fuel to the fire

   _____

How to: _____

A **procedure** is a set of steps to follow to make or do something. For example, recipes and instructions are types of procedures.

Description:

_____

Materials or ingredients:

_____   _____   _____

_____   _____   _____

_____   _____   _____

Instructions:

_____

_____

_____

_____

_____

_____

_____

_____

_____

☐ I have a description that tells what you will make or do.

☐ The information is organized under headings.

☐ Each step has a number.

☐ I used action words to tell which actions to do.

☐ I checked for correct spelling and punctuation.

☐ I used sequencing words such as _first_, _next_, _then_, and _finally_.

Write a Letter of Advice

Dear _____,

GREETING

DATE

BODY

_____

_____

_____

_____

_____

_____

_____

_____

_____

_____

_____

_____

_____

Sincerely,

☐ **Capitalization**
☐ **Organization**
☐ **Punctuation**
☐ **Spelling**

_____

CLOSING / SIGNATURE

Title: _____

(blank writing box)

_____

_____

_____

_____

_____

_____

_____

_____

☐ **C**apitalization   • Do my sentences and proper nouns have capital letters?

☐ **O**rganization   • Did I order my ideas in a way that makes sense?

☐ **P**unctuation   • Do my sentences have end marks?   (**.!?**)

☐ **S**pelling   • Did I check my spelling to the best of my ability?

Write a Funny Dialogue

Write a dialogue between two friends. Remember to use quotation marks.

_____

_____

_____

_____

_____

_____

_____

_____

_____

_____

_____

_____

_____

_____

☐ I put quotation marks around all the words that someone said.

☐ I included speaker tags before or after the spoken words.

☐ I used commas with speaker tags before or after the spoken words.

☐ I did not use commas with question marks or exclamation marks.

☐ I started the first word with a capital when the speaker tag came first.

☐ I made my dialogue interesting and natural.

Cinquain Poem

A **cinquain** is a poem that has five lines. Use the lines below to write cinquain poems about a person, place, or thing.

Line 1: two syllables

_____

Line 2: four syllables

_____

Line 3: six syllables

_____

Line 4: eight syllables

_____

Line 5: two syllables

_____

Line 1: two syllables

_____

Line 2: four syllables

_____

Line 3: six syllables

_____

Line 4: eight syllables

_____

Line 5: two syllables

_____

☐ I used interesting words.   ☐ I checked for correct spelling and punctuation.

Haiku Poem

Haiku is a traditional style of Japanese poetry. Usually, haiku poems have a nature theme, such as animals or the seasons. Haiku poems are a good way to describe something.

Haiku poems have only three lines. There are five syllables in its first line, seven syllables in its second line, and five syllables in its third line. The third line is usually a subject that is only slightly connected to the first two lines.

Example: Leaves blow in the wind
Skies darken and thunder booms.
The rain helps things grow.

Write your own **haiku**.

1. Choose a subject for your haiku. Brainstorm a list of words about your subject. Beside each word, note how many syllables it has.

2. Choose a second subject for the last line of your haiku. It should remind the reader of the subject.

_____

3. Write your haiku.

Line 1 (5 syllables) _____

Line 2 (7 syllables) _____

Line 3 (5 syllables) _____

Brochure Checklist

A **brochure** is a booklet or pamphlet that contains descriptive information.

Topic: _____

Purpose: ☐ to give information   ☐ to persuade   ☐ to entertain

STEP 1: Plan Your Brochure

☐ Fold a piece of paper the same way your brochure will be folded. Before writing the brochure, plan the layout in pencil. Sections of the brochure will include:

_____   _____

_____   _____

☐ Write the heading for each section where you would like it to be in the brochure.

☐ Plan where graphics or pictures will be placed in the brochure.

STEP 2: Complete a Draft

☐ Research information for each section of your brochure. Check your facts.

☐ Read your draft for meaning, then add, delete, or change words to make your writing better.

☐ Plan what illustrations or graphics you will put into your brochure.

STEP 3: Checklist

☐ My brochure is neat and well organized.

☐ My brochure has accurate information.

☐ My brochure has pictures or graphics that go well with the information.

☐ I checked the spelling and grammar.

☐ I checked the punctuation.

☐ My brochure is attractive.

Use a computer to create a digital version of your brochure!

Narrative Writing Planner

Narrative writing tells a story that has a beginning, a middle, and an end. It can be about something that actually happened or it can be made up.

Title: _____

Characters	Setting / Mood

Conflict / Problem	Resolution / Ending

Beginning

Middle

End

Write your narrative on a separate piece of paper or digitally.

Folktales

Folktales are stories that have been passed on from generation to generation, usually to teach a lesson. Often folktales take place in a magic kingdom, dark forest, village, or similar setting. The problem in a folktale is often solved with great deeds or remarkable kindness.

Folktales also often include

- magic events, characters, or objects
- clear good and wicked characters
- talking animals
- a happy ending
- the number 3
- repeat phrases

Examples: King Midas   The Three Little Pigs

Read a **folktale**. How do you know it is a folktale? Explain your thinking with reasons and examples.

Title: _____

_____

_____

_____

_____

_____

_____

_____

Folktale Writing Planner

Write ideas for your folktale. Use this planner to help you.

Lesson: Decide what lesson your folktale will teach.

Characters: Which characters will be good? Which characters will be wicked? Think about how you will let your readers know which is which.

Setting: Where and when will your folktale take place? **Hint:** Folktales often begin with "Once upon a time..." or "Long, long, ago..."

Importance of 3: How will the number 3 be included in your folktale?

Problem: What is the problem to be solved in your folktale?

Patterning & Algebra Checklist

Expectations	Not Yet	Developing	Proficient	Mastered
create, identify, and extend numeric and geometric patterns, using a variety of tools				
make predictions related to growing and shrinking geometric and numeric patterns				
determine the missing number in equations involving addition, subtraction, multiplication, or division and one- or two-digit numbers				
make a table of values for a pattern that is generated by adding or subtracting a number to get to the next term				
extend and create repeating patterns that result from translations, through investigation using a variety of tools				
demonstrate through investigation, an understanding of variables as unknown quantities represented by a letter or other symbol				

Not Yet: rarely applies skills, several errors or omissions

Developing: sometimes applies skills, some errors or omissions

Proficient: usually applies skills, few errors or omissions

Mastered: consistently applies skills, almost no errors or omissions

Number Concepts Checklist

Expectations	Not Yet	Developing	Proficient	Mastered
read and order whole numbers to 100 000, decimal numbers to hundredths, proper and improper fractions, and mixed numbers				
demonstrate an understanding of magnitude by counting forward and backwards by 0.01				
represent, compare, and order whole numbers and decimal numbers from 0.01 to 100 000				
read and print in words whole numbers to ten thousand				
round decimal numbers to the nearest tenth				
explain the concept of equivalent fractions				
read and write money amounts to $1000				
count forward by hundredths from any decimal number expressed to two decimal places				
solve problems involving the addition, subtraction, and multiplication of whole numbers				
add and subtract decimal numbers to hundredths, including money amounts				
multiply two-digit whole numbers by two-digit whole numbers				
divide three-digit whole numbers by one-digit whole numbers				
multiply decimal numbers by 10, 100, 1000, and 10 000, and divide decimal numbers by 10 and 100				

Not Yet: rarely applies skills, several errors or omissions

Developing: sometimes applies skills, some errors or omissions

Proficient: usually applies skills, few errors or omissions

Mastered: consistently applies skills, almost no errors or omissions

Data Management and Probability Checklist

Expectations	Not Yet	Developing	Proficient	Mastered
distinguish between discrete data and continuous data				
collect data by conducting a survey or an experiment to do with themselves, their environment, issues in their school or community, or content from another subject, and record observations or measurements				
collect and organize discrete or continuous primary data and secondary data, and display the data in charts, graphs, or tables that have appropriate titles, labels, and scales that suit the range and distribution of the data, using a variety of tools				
demonstrate an understanding that sets of data can be samples of larger populations				
describe, through investigation, how a set of data is collected and explain whether the collection method is appropriate				
read, interpret, and draw conclusions from primary data				
compare similarities and differences between two related sets of data, using a variety of strategies				
calculate the mean for a small set of data and use it to describe the shape of the data set across its range of values, using charts, tables, and graphs				
represent, using a common fraction, the probability that an event will occur				
determine and represent all the possible outcomes in a simple probability experiment				

Not Yet: rarely applies skills, several errors or omissions

Developing: sometimes applies skills, some errors or omissions

Proficient: usually applies skills, few errors or omissions

Mastered: consistently applies skills, almost no errors or omissions

Measurement Checklist

Expectations	Not Yet	Developing	Proficient	Mastered
estimate, measure, and represent time intervals to the nearest second				
estimate and determine elapsed time, with and without using a timeline, given the durations of events expressed in minutes, hours, days, weeks, months, or years				
estimate and measure the perimeter and area of regular and irregular polygons, using a variety of tools				
select and justify the most appropriate standard unit to measure length, height, width, and distance, and to measure the perimeter of various polygons				
solve problems requiring conversion from metres to centimetres, and from kilometres to metres				
solve problems involving the relationship between a 12-hour clock and a 24-hour clock				
solve problems requiring the estimation and calculation of perimeters and areas of rectangles				
select and justify the most appropriate standard unit to measure mass				
determine through investigation, the relationship between capacity and volume by comparing the volume of an object with the amount of liquid it can contain or displace				

Not Yet: rarely applies skills, several errors or omissions

Developing: sometimes applies skills, some errors or omissions

Proficient: usually applies skills, few errors or omissions

Mastered: consistently applies skills, almost no errors or omissions

Geometry and Spatial Sense Checklist

Expectations	Not Yet	Developing	Proficient	Mastered
distinguish among polygons, regular polygons, and other two-dimensional shapes				
distinguish among prisms, right prisms, pyramids, and other three-dimensional figures				
identify and classify acute, right, obtuse, and straight angles				
measure and construct angles up to 90°, using a protractor				
identify triangles and classify them according to angle and side properties				
construct triangles, using a variety of tools, given acute or right angles and side measurements				
identify prisms and pyramids from their nets				
construct nets of prisms and pyramids using a variety of tools				
locate an object using the cardinal directions				
compare grid systems commonly used on maps				
identify, perform, and describe translations using a variety of tools				
create and analyze designs by translating and/or reflecting a shape, or shapes, using a variety of tools				

Not Yet: rarely applies skills, several errors or omissions

Developing: sometimes applies skills, some errors or omissions

Proficient: usually applies skills, few errors or omissions

Mastered: consistently applies skills, almost no errors or omissions

MONDAY — Patterning and Algebra

1 Which property does this equation show?

3 + 7 = 7 + 3

A. commutative

B. associative

C. distributive

3 Solve for *k*.

21 + *k* = 44

2 Extend the pattern.

4 What is the pattern rule?

9, 18, 27, 36, 45, 54

TUESDAY — Number Sense

1 Fill in the blank to compare the numbers.

400 is _____ times larger than 40

2 32 × 10 =

3 Which number is greater than 72 898 and less than 73 889?

A. 73 635

B. 73 992

4 Add. Use words, pictures, or equations to show your work.

0.3 + 0.5 + 0.8 =

WEDNESDAY · Fractions and Decimals

1 Write two equivalent fractions.

$\dfrac{2}{4}$

2 Write the decimal as fraction.

a) 0.3   ——

b) 0. 25   ——

3 Compare the fraction to the number using <, >, or =.

$\dfrac{30}{7}$ ☐ 5

4 Write the mixed number as an improper fraction.

$4 \dfrac{6}{9}$

THURSDAY · Geometry and Spatial Sense

1 Write the coordinate pair for each item on the coordinate plane.

★ _____   ⊕ _____   ◆ _____

_____   _____   _____

_____   _____   _____

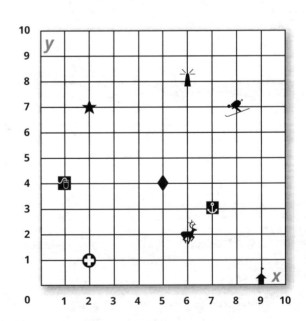

2 Draw a circle at (4, 9).

3 Draw a triangle at (0, 5).

1 Fill in the blank.

1 t = 1000 kg

1 kg = _____ g

1 g = _____ mg

2 Which 3D figure would you use to measure the volume of a box?

A.

B.

C.

3 Which container will hold more liquid: a 3-litre container or a 3000-millilitre container?

4 The time is 10:35 a.m. What time will it be in 285 minutes?

BRAIN STRETCH

A box of cookies weighs 520 grams. Amanda brought three boxes to the class party. What is the combined weight of the boxes in kilograms?

MONDAY — Patterning and Algebra

1 Extend the pattern.

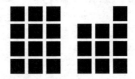

2 Compare the expressions without calculating. Use <, >, or =.

22 + 11 + 33 ☐ 11 + 22 + 33

3 What are the next two terms of the pattern?

○☐   ○☐○   ○☐○☐

4 What is the pattern rule?

6, 12, 24, 48, 96

TUESDAY — Number Sense

1 6 hundreds = _____ ones

2 80 × 100 =

3 Compare the decimals using <, >, or =.

0.67 ☐ 0.67

4 Subtract. Use words, pictures, or equations to show your work.

10 − 7.4 =

WEDNESDAY — Fractions and Decimals

1 Write two equivalent fractions.

$$\frac{1}{8}$$

2 Compare the fractions using <, >, or =.

$$\frac{6}{8} \quad \boxed{} \quad \frac{1}{8}$$

3 Write the improper fraction as a mixed number.

$$\frac{15}{8}$$

4 Represent the fraction using the shapes.

$$\frac{9}{4}$$

THURSDAY — Geometry and Spatial Sense

1 Circle all the polygons.

2 Colour the regular polygons green.

3 Colour the irregular polygons blue.

4 Choose one shape that is not a polygon. Describe how you could change it into a polygon.

1 A garbage truck has the mass of 10 tonnes. What is the mass in kg?

2 A rug is $2\frac{1}{2}$ metres long. How long is the rug in centimetres?

3 Calculate the volume of the box.

a)  _____

b)  _____

c) 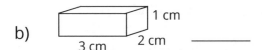 _____

4 What is the volume of this shape in cubic units? _____

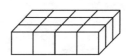

BRAIN STRETCH

The city of Oakdale wants students to walk in the annual parade and throw candy to the crowds. The city wants one student with the first float, two students with the second float, three students with the third float, four students with the fourth float, and so on. There are 10 floats in the parade. If the pattern continues, how many students in total will walk in the parade?

MONDAY — Patterning and Algebra

1 Which property does this equation show?

$8 \times 60 = 60 \times 8$

A. distributive

B. associative

C. commutative

3 Create a growing geometric pattern.

2 Find the missing number in the equation.

$60 = 72 - \underline{\hspace{1cm}}$

4 What is the pattern rule?

1000, 950, 900, 850, 800

TUESDAY — Number Sense

1 Write the number in standard form.

a) $30\ 000 + 600 + 70 + 5 =$

b) twenty four thousand twelve =

3 Fill in the blank to compare the numbers.

0.5 is _____ times smaller than 5

2 a) Complete the pattern.

$3 \times 1 = \underline{\hspace{2cm}}$

$3 \times 10 = \underline{\hspace{2cm}}$

$3 \times 100 = \underline{\hspace{2cm}}$

$3 \times 1000 = \underline{\hspace{2cm}}$

b) Find $3 \times 100\ 000$ without multiplying.

4 Subtract. Use words, pictures, or equations to show your work.

$20.5 - 5.4 =$

1 Write the improper fraction as a mixed number.

$$\frac{5}{3}$$

2 Add.

$$\frac{5}{8} + \frac{3}{4}$$

4 How many tenths are in 6.7?

3 Compare the fraction to the number using <, >, or =.

$$\frac{3}{4} \boxed{} 1$$

1 Classify the pair of lines

A. intersecting

B. perpendicular

C. parallel

2 Which shapes are polygons?

A.   B.   C.   D.

3 Draw an irregular polygon with 6 sides.

4 How many lines of symmetry are there?

P _____

1 What is a reasonable amount of time to brush your teeth?

   A. 2 minutes

   B. 2 seconds

   C. 2 hours

2 Olivia was in a track and field competition. In the long jump event, she jumped 4.45 metres. How many centimetres did she jump?

3 A box has a volume of eighteen cubic metres. Which is the correct way to write the volume?

   A. 18 m   B. 18 m^2 C. 18 m^3

4 Thomas put 30 unit cubes in a box like this:

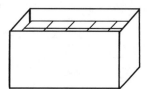

He says the volume of the box is 30 cubic units. Is this correct? Why or why not?

BRAIN STRETCH

Helen made 6 pizzas and cut each of them into eighths.
If she served $3\frac{1}{4}$ pizzas, how many slices of pizza did Helen have left over?

MONDAY — Patterning and Algebra

1 Which expression is **not** equal to 5 × 5?

   A. 5 + 5 + 5 + 5 + 5

   B. 4 × 5 + 5

   C. 2 × 5

   D. 5 + 4 × 5

2 Create a growing numeric pattern that includes multiplication.

Pattern rule: _____

3 Complete the function table.
Rule: Output = Input × 12

Input	Output
3	
6	
9	
12	
15	

4 Write an algebraic expression.

20 more than 17

TUESDAY — Number Sense

1 _____ hundreds = 40 tens

2 To which place value was the number rounded?

67 874 → 68 000

_____

3 a) Complete the pattern.

     50 ÷ 10 = ____

   500 ÷ 10 = ____

  5000 ÷ 10 = ____

50 000 ÷ 10 = ____

b) Find 90 000 ÷ 10 without dividing.

4 List the factors for 48.

WEDNESDAY — Fractions and Decimals

1 Write two equivalent fractions.

$$\frac{5}{10}$$

2 Write the mixed number as an improper fraction.

$$6\,\frac{2}{3}$$

3 Compare the quantities using <, >, or =.

$$3 \times \frac{3}{4} \boxed{} 3$$

4 Sebastian and his family picked $4\frac{1}{3}$ bushels of red apples and $2\frac{1}{8}$ bushels of green apples. How many bushels of apples did the family pick in all? Draw a model or write an equation to show your work.

THURSDAY — Geometry and Spatial Sense

1 Write the coordinate pair for each point.

A _____   B _____   C _____

D _____   E _____   F _____

G _____   H _____   I _____

2 Draw a point at (2, 2).

3 Draw a point at (0, 3).

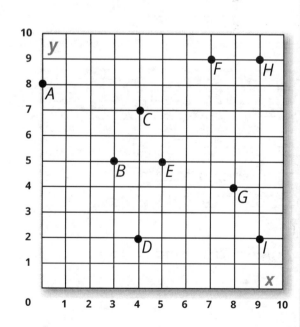

Measurement and Data

Jane asked all the students in her class how many times they visited the library to get research materials for a class project. This is the data she collected:

Number of Visits to the Library

1 2 0 2 4 2 0 2 2 2 4 2 3 3 3 4 4 4 3 4 4 2 4 4

1 Use Jane's data to complete the line plot.

$\longleftarrow$|⎯⎯⎯⎯⎯|⎯⎯⎯⎯⎯|⎯⎯⎯⎯⎯|⎯⎯⎯⎯⎯|$\longrightarrow$

2 What can you conclude from the line plot?

_____

_____

BRAIN STRETCH

Use a coloured pencil to draw the translation. **Hint:** Use arrows to show the distance and the direction.

2 units to the right and 4 units down

MONDAY — Patterning and Algebra

1 Solve for *m*.

$m \times 12 = 144$

2 Create a shrinking geometric pattern.

3 What is the pattern rule?

67, 73, 77, 83, 87

4 Circle the numbers that are **not** a multiple of 12.

144   24   56   36   96

TUESDAY — Number Sense

1 What is the value of 2 in each number?

a) 742 _____

b) 724 _____

2 How much money do you have?

3 Order from least to greatest.

109, 567, 23, 876

4 Add. Use words, pictures, or equations to show your work.

$50.24 + 10.5 =$

WEDNESDAY — Fractions and Decimals

1 Subtract, then simplify your answer.

$$\frac{5}{6} - \frac{1}{3}$$

2 Compare the fraction to the number using <, >, or =.

$$\frac{21}{2} \; \boxed{} \; 10$$

3 Write the decimal as fraction.

a) 0.75 —

b) 0.2 —

4 Plot $\frac{6}{8}$ on the number line.
Is it closest to 0, $\frac{1}{2}$, or 1?

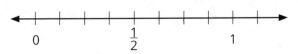

0          $\frac{1}{2}$ 1

THURSDAY — Geometry and Spatial Sense

1 Classify the pair of lines.

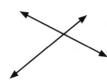

A. intersecting

B. perpendicular

C. parallel

2 Draw and name 2 polygons that have more than 4 sides.

3 What is the general term for a polygon that has four sides?

4 Choose all the words that describe this shape.

A. parallelogram

B. rhombus

C. quadrilateral

D. square

1 100 years = _____ months

2 Sharon walked 2 metres to the beach. How many decimetres did she walk?

3 What are the perimeter and area of a tabletop that is 56 cm wide and 80 cm long?

4 What is the volume of this shape in cubic units?

_____

BRAIN STRETCH

Adele has to be at school by 8:30 a.m. It takes her 15 minutes to get dressed, 10 minutes to eat, and 25 minutes to walk to school. What time should she get up?

MONDAY — Patterning and Algebra

1 Create a shrinking numeric pattern.

Pattern rule: _____

2 Complete the function table.
Rule: Output = Input ÷ 8

Input	Output
8	
88	
32	
64	
16	

3 Classify the numbers as prime (P) or composite (C).

a) 39 _____

b) 87 _____

4 Solve.

a) $z + 9 = 25$ $z =$

b) $25 - y = 14$ $y =$

TUESDAY — Number Sense

1 a) $34 \times 1 =$ _____

b) $34 \times 10 =$ _____

c) $340 \times 100 =$ _____

d) What do you notice about the number of zeroes in the product when you multiply by powers of 10?

3 How many tenths are in 1.5?

2 Which is more money?

A. $5.00 bill, 2 loonies, 3 quarters, 2 dimes

B. $5.00 bill, 1 toonie, 4 quarters, 5 dimes, 1 nickel

4 Compare using <, >, or =.

0.450 ☐ 0.451

WEDNESDAY — Fractions and Decimals

1 Write two equivalent fractions.

$\dfrac{4}{7}$

2 Compare the quantities using <, >, or =.

$2\dfrac{1}{4}$ ☐ $\dfrac{12}{4}$

3 Write an improper fraction and a mixed fraction.

4 Which is greater, $\dfrac{4}{3}$ or $\dfrac{3}{4}$?

Use the number lines.

```
0        1        2        3        4
+--+--+--+--+--+--+--+--+--+--+--+--+
```

```
0        1        2        3        4
+--+--+--+--+--+--+--+--+--+--+--+--+
```

THURSDAY — Geometry and Spatial Sense

1 Write the coordinate pair for each point.

A _____ B _____ C _____

D _____ E _____ F _____

G _____ H _____ I _____

2 Draw a point at (0, 0).

3 Draw a point at (8, 1).

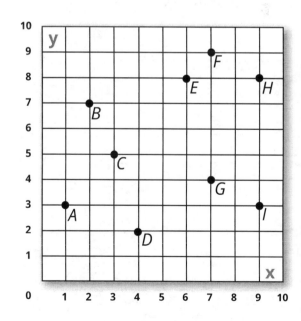

FRIDAY — Measurement and Data

1 What metric unit would be best to measure the distance from your home to school?

2 Convert the measurement

a) 3 km = _____ m

d) 150 cm = _____ mm

b) 8 m = _____ cm

3 Connor trained for the track meet by running 2.4 km every day. How many metres did he run every week?

4 What is the volume of this shape in cubic units?

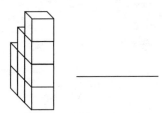

_____

BRAIN STRETCH

Name the angle. Choose from right, acute, obtuse, and straight angles.

a) _____

b) _____

c) _____

d) _____

e) _____

f) _____

g) _____

h) _____

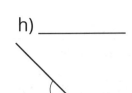

Patterning and Algebra

1 Replace the variable with the given number and solve. $b = 2$

a) $6 + b =$

b) $20 - b =$

3 What is the pattern rule?

5, 10, 20, 40, 80, 160

2 Complete the function table.
Rule: Output = Input × 9

Input	Output
7	
6	
10	
11	
4	

4 Compare the expressions using <, >, or =.

$60 + 2$ ☐ $10 × 6$

Number Sense

1 9 hundreds = _____ ones

2 Write the number in expanded form.

a) 87 451 _____

b) 18 380 _____

3 Complete the sentence using <, >, or =.

$9.3 - 0.2$ ☐ 9.1

4 Multiply. Use words, pictures, or equations to show your work.

$5.5 × 10 =$

1 Add.

$$\frac{2}{3} + \frac{1}{9} =$$

2 Compare the quantities using <, >, or =.

$$2\frac{1}{4} \boxed{} \frac{12}{4}$$

3 Write as a decimal.

a) four and three tenths _____

b) two and five tenths _____

c) $\frac{40}{100}$ _____

4 Charlie had $4\frac{1}{2}$ cups of tomato sauce in a large can. He used three quarters of a cup to make spaghetti sauce. How much tomato sauce is left in the large can?

THURSDAY — Geometry and Spatial Sense

1 Use the words below to complete the chart.

	3D Figure	Name of 3D Figure	Number of Faces	Number of Edges	Number of Vertices
a)					
b)					
c)					
d)					

This double bar graph shows how many tulips of each colour Chris and Sophie planted in their gardens.

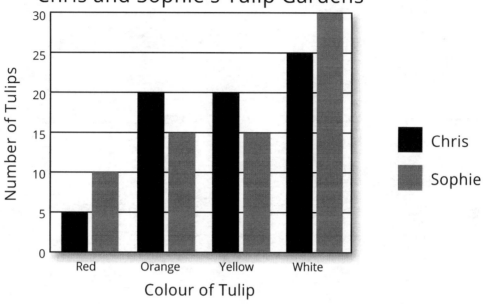

Chris and Sophie's Tulip Gardens

1 How many red tulips did Sophie plant? _____

2 How many fewer white tulips did Chris plant than Sophie? _____

3 Who planted more orange and yellow tulips? _____

4 Who planted the most tulips altogether, Chris or Sophie? Estimate by looking at the graph. Then add the totals to check your estimate.

_____

BRAIN STRETCH

A hotel has a pool in the shape of a rectangle. The pool is 8 m long, 3 m wide, and 2000 cm deep. What is the volume of the pool in cubic metres?

MONDAY — Patterning and Algebra

1 Which expression is equal to 6 × 42?

A. 6 × (42 − 2)
B. 6 × (6 + 42)
C. 6 × (40 − 2)
D. 6 × (40 + 2)

3 Compare the expressions without calculating. Use <, >, or =.

(4 × 4) × 2 [ ] 4 × (4 × 2)

2 Find the rule and complete the function table.

Input	Output
5	55
6	
7	77
8	88
9	

4 Write an algebraic expression for:

75 reduced by 25

TUESDAY — Number Sense

1 Regroup to solve.

4 × 50 = 4 × _____ tens = _____ tens = _____

2 How much money is 50 toonies?

3 Subtract. Use words, pictures, or equations to show your work.

0.50 − 0.44

4   75
       × 36

Fractions and Decimals

1 Write two equivalent fractions.

$$\frac{10}{22}$$

2 Write the mixed number as an improper fraction.

$$5\frac{1}{8}$$

3 Compare the fraction to the number using <, >, or =.

$$\frac{14}{2} \boxed{} 7$$

4 At a party, 12 people shared 2 apple pies equally. What fraction of pie did each person get? Show your work using pictures, words, and numbers.

THURSDAY **Geometry and Spatial Sense**

1 Count the number of sides in each shape.

A ___ sides   B ___ sides   C ___ sides   D ___ sides

E ___ sides   F ___ sides   G ___ sides   H ___ sides

I ___ sides

J ___ sides

2 Sort the shapes. The first one is done for you.

Category	Shape
Quadrilaterals	
Not Quadrilaterals	A

1 3 quarter hours = _____ minutes

2 Brian rides his bike to and from school each day. The distance from his house to the school is 1.8 km.
a) How many metres does Brian ride each day? _____
b) How many metres does he ride in five days? _____

3 Calculate the perimeter of the rectangle.

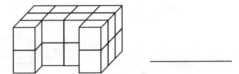

12.2 units

5.1 units

4 What is the volume of this shape in cubic units?

_____

BRAIN STRETCH

Choose the correct net for each 3D figure.

a)
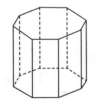

A.

B.
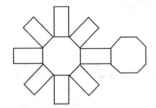

a)
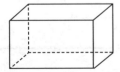

A.
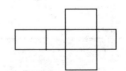

B.
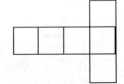

MONDAY — Patterning and Algebra

1 Solve.

a) $24 = 12r$ $r =$

b) $x = 72 - 23$ $x =$

2 Predict what the 27th figure will be in this pattern.

A. △   B. ▽   C. ◁

3 How many times larger or smaller? Compare the expressions without calculating.

$9 \times (730 - 144)$ is _____ times

_____ than $(730 - 144) \times 3$

4 Write an algebraic expression.

add 12 and 8, then divide by 2

TUESDAY — Number Sense

1 _____ tens = 400 ones

2 Each digit is 4, but the value is different.

a) How does the 4 that the arrow points to compare in value to the 4 to its left?

b) How does it compare in value to the 4 to its right?

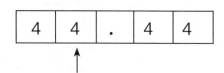

3 Complete the sentence using <, >, or =.

$5.3 + 2.3$ ☐ 8

4 Fill in the blank.

_____ is 100 more than 684

WEDNESDAY — Fractions and Decimals

1 Write the improper fraction as a mixed number.

$$\frac{24}{9}$$

2 Add, then simplify your answer.

$$\frac{2}{12} + \frac{4}{5} =$$

3 Compare the quantities using <, >, or =.

$4\frac{3}{4}$ ☐ $\frac{20}{4}$

4 If you have 4 apples and I have 6 apples, how many more do I have? Write the answer as a decimal and a fraction.

THURSDAY — Geometry and Spatial Sense

1 Classify the pair of lines

A. intersecting

B. perpendicular

C. parallel

2 How are a square and a parallelogram alike?

3 Choose all the words that describe the shape.

A. right

B. equilateral

C. triangle

D. scalene

4 Are these shapes congruent or similar?

1 Convert from centimetres to millimetres.

a) 12.5 cm

b) 40.5 cm

2 Jerry can type 25 words per minute. At this rate, how many words can Jerry type in 4.5 minutes?

3 Which room has a larger area and perimeter? Justify your answer.

Room A: 12 metres by 8 metres

Room B: 9 metres by 9 metres

4 a) What is the volume of this shape in cubic units?

_____

b) What would be the total volume of 4 shapes like this one?

_____

BRAIN STRETCH

At 6:30 a.m., the outdoor temperature was 16°C. Between 6:30 a.m. and 11:30 a.m., the temperature increased by 3°C. What was the temperature at 11:30 a.m.?

MONDAY — Patterning and Algebra

1 Solve.

a) $64 = 8r$ $r =$

b) $x = 42 \div 7$ $x =$

2 Complete the function table.
Rule: Output = Input ÷ 5 × 10

Input	Output
45	
60	
5	
15	
30	

4 Which expression is **not** equal to 32?

A. $4 \times 4 \times 2$

B. 4×8

C. $2 \times 4 \times 4$

D. 8×2

3 Write an algebraic expression.

add 6 and 5, then multiply by 3

TUESDAY — Number Sense

1 10 hundred thousands

= _____ ten thousands

2 For the number 3333, the 3 in the tens place represents 30.

a) The 3 in the hundreds place represents_____.

b) The 3 in the thousands place represents _____.

c) The 3 in the hundreds place is _____ times as much as the 3 in the tens place.

3 Round each number to the nearest whole number and the nearest tenth.

a)   7. 25

b)   0.89

4 Divide. Use words, pictures, or equations to show your work.

$35.5 \div 5 =$

WEDNESDAY — Fractions and Decimals

1 Subtract.

$$\frac{8}{9} - \frac{3}{5} =$$

2 Compare the fraction to the number using <, >, or =.

$$\frac{7}{6} \ \boxed{} \ 2$$

3 Order the decimals from least to greatest.

a) 3.94, 3.65, 1.33 _____

b) 0.5, 0.99, 0.25 _____

4 Ashley used $6\frac{6}{8}$ centimetres of red ribbon and $7\frac{1}{4}$ centimetres of white ribbon to wrap a present. How many centimetres of ribbon did Ashley use altogether?

THURSDAY — Geometry and Spatial Sense

1 Plot the points on the coordinate plane.

A (2, 2)	E (6, 6)
B (4, 5)	F (0, 9)
C (7, 9)	G (4, 4)
D (1, 3)	H (8, 8)

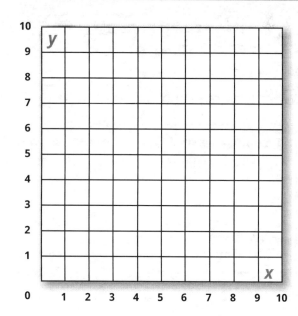

2 a) Which points have the same x-coordinate? _____
   b) Which points have the same y-coordinate? _____

3 Draw a line between points A and F. Which other points are on the line? _____

This pictograph shows the amount of ice cream sold at the ice cream parlour on the weekend.

Ice Cream Sold (in scoops)

Chocolate	🍦🍦🍦🍦🍦
Chocolate Chip	🍦🍦🍦🍦🍦🍦🍦🍦🍦
Strawberry	🍦🍦🍦🍦🍦🍦🍦🍦🍦🍦🍦
Vanilla	🍦🍦🍦🍦🍦🍦🍦

Key: 🍦 = 2 scoops

1 How many scoops of each flavour were sold?

2 What is the mean number of scoops per flavour and the range of ice cream scoops sold?

3 What kind of graph would you use to show the trend of ice cream sold?

A. line graph   B. bar graph

BRAIN STRETCH

What type of graph would you use to display the following data?

1. comparing students' favourite colours	2. showing how a person spent $100	3. comparing students' hair colour
4. showing the price of a stock over a month	5. comparing students' favourite television shows	6. showing the growth of a plant over six weeks

Patterning and Algebra

1 Add and subtract in order from left to right.

a) 4 + 5 – 6 = _____

b) 15 – 3 + 6 + 10 = _____

c) 12 – 5 – 2 + 9 + 10 = _____

3 Write an algebraic expression.

add 8 and 56, then divide by 4

2 Find the rule and complete the function table.

Rule: _____

Input	Output
4	400
7	700
8	
10	
	1100

4 Add brackets to make the equation true.

16 + 4 × 8 – 1 = 140

Number Sense

1 Which number would be rounded to 7000?

2 What is the greatest and least possible number using the following digits?

5 6 1 9 2

a) greatest: _____

b) least: _____

3 Complete the sentence using <, >, or =.

4.7 – 0.5 ☐ 4.5

4
```
   96
 × 61
```

WEDNESDAY — Fractions and Decimals

1 Write two equivalent fractions.

$$\frac{3}{5}$$

2 Write the improper fraction as a mixed number.

$$\frac{14}{13}$$

3 Each square in the grid has sides that measure $\frac{1}{4}$ cm. What is the area of the rectangle in centimetres?

4 Mrs. Mudhar needs at least 16 metres of fabric to make costumes. She has $4\frac{1}{2}$ metres of fabric at home and she buys $10\frac{1}{3}$ metres of the same fabric at the store. Does she have enough fabric for the costumes? Justify your answer.

THURSDAY — Geometry and Spatial Sense

1 Which shape is **not** a quadrilateral?

A. octagon

B. rhombus

C. square

2 Classify the triangle. Circle all the descriptions that apply.

B
70°
60°   50°
A   C

A. acute

B. isosceles

C. obtuse

D. scalene

E. right

3 How many lines of symmetry are there?

X _____

4 Are these shapes congruent or similar?

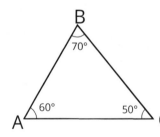

1 Identify each as continuous data or discrete data.

a) arm span

b) age in years

c) time it takes to get to school

2 Give your own example of

a) continous data

b) discrete data

3 Fill in the blank.

first-hand   second-hand

a) Data that you collect yourself is _____ data.

b) Data that someone else collected is _____ data.

4 Classify as first-hand or second-hand data.

a) how far students in Grade 5 can jump

b) the height of a bean plant as it grows

BRAIN STRETCH

Carlos went shopping for cereal. Honey Hoops cereal costs $1.50/500 g and Fruity Flakes cereal costs $0.55/100 g. Which cereal is the better buy? Show your reasoning.

MONDAY — Patterning and Algebra

1 Which expression is equal to 4×60 ?

A. 4×55
B. 24×10
C. 240×5

3 Write an algebraic expression.

subtract 5 from 11, then add 2

2 a) Extend the pattern.

1 2 1 1 3 1 1 1 4 1 1 1 1 5 ___ ___ ___

b) What kind of the pattern is this?

A. repeating B. shrinking C. growing

4 Replace the variable with the given number and solve. $h = 8$

a) $7 \times h =$

b) $72 \div h =$

TUESDAY — Number Sense

1 Round each number to the nearest whole number and the nearest tenth.

a)   0.27

b)   4.06

2 Complete the sentence using <, >, or =.

$2.4 + 0.5$ ☐ 3.9

3 Multiply. Use words, pictures, or equations to show your work.

$15.9 \times 4 =$

4 Divide. Use words, pictures, or equations to show your work

$88 \div 2 =$

WEDNESDAY — Fractions and Decimals

1 Add. Show your work.

$$3\frac{5}{6} + 5\frac{2}{3} =$$

2 Add.

$$\frac{1}{7} + \frac{5}{7} =$$

3 Plot $\frac{1}{8}$ on the number line. Is it closest to 0, $\frac{1}{2}$, or 1?

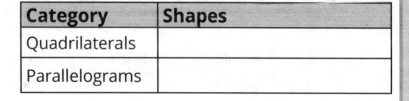

4 Write a decimal for the fraction.

$$\frac{4}{10}$$

THURSDAY — Geometry and Spatial Sense

1 Sort the shapes below into the chart.

Category	Shapes
Quadrilaterals	
Parallelograms	

2 Which shapes do not belong in either group?

_____

1 Use the graph to answer the questions.

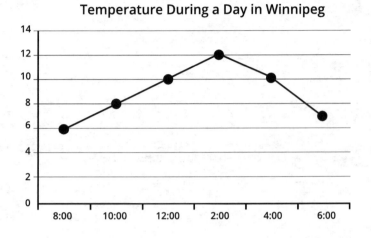

Temperature During a Day in Winnipeg

a) What was the highest temperature?

b) What was the lowest temperature?

c) What is the difference between the high and low temperature?

d) What was the temperature at 4:00?

e) About how warm was it at 1:00?

f) Does this graph show continuous data or discrete data?

BRAIN STRETCH

George has a paper airplane that can fly 3.6 m. His friend Paul has one that can go 246 cm. Whose paper airplane can fly farther? How much farther can that person's airplane fly in centimetres?

MONDAY — Patterning and Algebra

1 a) Write the first five terms of each pattern.

Start at 1 and add 2 each time.

____, ____, ____, ____, ____

Start at 1 and add 3 each time.

____, ____, ____, ____, ____

b) Compare the two patterns. What do you notice?

_____

_____

2 Replace the variable with the given number and solve.

$h = 5$

a) $25 - h =$

b) $7h + 5 =$

3 Write an algebraic expression for:

b increased by 11

TUESDAY — Number Sense

1 _____ hundreds = 30 000 ones

2 Write the number in standard form.

a) $70\ 000 + 3000 + 80 + 2 =$

b) eighty thousand five hundred twelve

3 Compare the decimals using <, >, or =.

0.99 ☐ 0.09

4 Multiply. Use words, pictures, or equations to show your work.

$6.3 \times 5 =$

WEDNESDAY — Fractions and Decimals

1 Add.

$$\frac{6}{7} + \frac{1}{14}$$

2 Write the mixed number as an improper fraction.

$$2\frac{4}{5}$$

3 Andrew goes to school for 5 days out of each week. What fraction of each week does Andrew not go to school?

4 Four friends shared 7 sandwiches equally. How many sandwiches did each friend eat? Express your answer as a fraction. Show your work using pictures, words, and numbers.

THURSDAY — Geometry and Spatial Sense

1 Use the words below to complete the chart.

3D Figure	Name of 3D Figure	Number of Faces	Number of Edges	Number of Vertices
a)				
b)				
c)				

Measurement and Data

1 Convert from centimetres to millimetres.

a)   5 cm

b)   13.2 cm

2 Choose the best unit of measurement to measure the height of a school.

A. mm   B. cm   cC.m

3 Corey was in a track and field competition. He completed the 2,000-metre walk in 9.5 minutes. About how many metres did he walk per minute?

4 a) Each cube has sides 1 cm. What is the total volume of the shape?

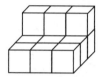

_____

b) What would be the total volume of 3 shapes like this one?

_____

BRAIN STRETCH

Jennifer saved $30. Last week, she spent half of her savings on new clothes and one eighth of her savings on music downloads. What fraction of her savings does she have left? How much money does she have left?

1. Complete the patterns. Start from 0. Add 2 each time. Add 1 each time.

a) _____, _____, _____, _____, _____

b) _____, _____, _____, _____, _____

2. Write the ordered pairs, using a) for the x-coordinate and b) for the y-coordinate. One is done for you.

1st term (____ , ____)

2nd term (_2_ , _1_)

3rd term (____ , ____)

4th term (____ , ____)

5th term (____ , ____)

3. Plot the ordered pairs on the coordinate plane and join the points. What do you see?

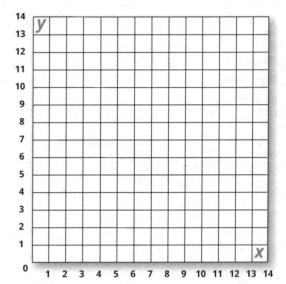

TUESDAY — Number Sense

1 How many dimes are in $100?

2 What is the place value of the 7 in 0.67?

3 Complete the sentence using <, >, or =.

9.6 ☐ 0.3 + 9.3

4 Write the numeral.

thirty-two thousand eight hundred ninety-six

5 Write the number that comes before and after the given number.

_____ 76 100 _____

WEDNESDAY — Fractions and Decimals

1 Add, then simplify your answer.

$$\frac{1}{2} + \frac{6}{7}$$

2 Write the mixed number as an improper fraction.

$$5\frac{3}{4}$$

3 Compare the quantities using <, >, or =.

$$5 \times \frac{1}{5} \ \boxed{} \ \frac{1}{5}$$

4 Represent the fraction using the circles.

$$\frac{10}{4}$$

THURSDAY — Geometry and Spatial Sense

1 Choose all the words that describe this shape.

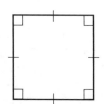

A. rectangle

B. quadrilateral

C. square

D. parallelogram

2 Which of these quadrilaterals are trapezoids?

A.   B.   C.

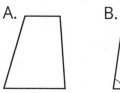

3 Draw an irregular polygon with 5 sides.

4 Draw and name a triangle that has no right angles.

Students at Elmwood School performed a play on four days.
This graph shows the number of tickets sold for each performance.

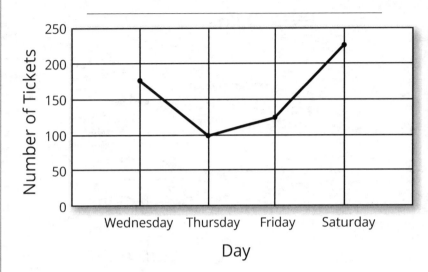

Day	Number of Tickets
Wednesday	
Thursday	
Friday	
Saturday	

1 Use the graph to complete the data table.

2 For which day were the most tickets sold? _____

3 What was the range of the number of tickets sold? _____

4 What was the increase in the number
of tickets sold from Friday to Saturday? _____

5 Add a title to the graph.

BRAIN STRETCH

Luke wants to bake ginger cookies, but he only wants to make half the recipe. The recipe calls for $1\frac{1}{3}$ cups of sugar. How much sugar should Luke use?

MONDAY — Patterning and Algebra

1 Replace the variable with the given number and solve.

$$p = 3$$

a) $27 \div p =$

b) $7p - 20 =$

3 Classify the numbers as prime (P) or composite (C).

a) 22 _____

b) 11 _____

2 Write an algebraic expression.

multiply the sum of 5 and 7 by the sum of 2 and 3

4 Find the prime factorization of 27.

TUESDAY — Number Sense

1 How many nickels are in $10?

3 Divide. Use words, pictures, or equations to show your work

$90 \div 3 =$

2 What is the place value of the 3 in each number?

a) 34 892 _____

b) 58 031 _____

4
$$\begin{array}{r} 3.8 \\ \times\ 4.9 \\ \hline \end{array}$$

1 Write the improper fraction as a mixed number.

$$\frac{34}{16}$$

2 Subtract, then simplify your answer.

$$\frac{6}{8} - \frac{2}{4} =$$

3 Write equivalent fractions but multiplying by a common factor.

$$\frac{1}{2} = \frac{}{4} = \frac{}{6} = \frac{}{8} = \frac{}{10}$$

4 Sarah bought $5\frac{1}{2}$ L of lemonade for a party. After the party, $2\frac{1}{4}$ L of lemonade were left. How much lemonade did the party guests drink?

THURSDAY — Geometry and Spatial Sense

1 Write translation, rotation, or reflection.

2 Create a design by translating a shape.

3 Create a design by rotating a shape.

4 Create a design by reflecting a shape.

1 Mike has a coin. What are the outcomes for flipping a coin?

2 Tess has 2 coins. Each coin has a head (H) and a tail (T). Write all the possible outcomes of tossing the two coins. Then write the number of possible outcomes.

_____

3 A spinner has 5 equal sections, 3 are blue and 2 are red. Lisa spins once. Find each probability. Write the answer as a fraction.

_____ possible outcomes

a) landing on blue _____

4 Using your answers for Question 2, what is the possibility of tossing 2 heads? Write it as a fraction.

b) landing on red _____

c) not landing on red _____

BRAIN STRETCH

A car left Sprucetown and travelled for 4 hours and 32 minutes to Pine City. Then the car travelled for 2 hours and 35 minutes, and arrived in Oakville at 3:30 p.m. What time did the car leave Sprucetown? Show your work.

MONDAY — Patterning and Algebra

1 a) Write the first five terms of each pattern.

Start at 12 and subtract 1 each time.

_____, _____, _____, _____, _____

Start at 12 and subtract 3 each time.

_____, _____, _____, _____, _____

b) Compare the two patterns. What do you notice?

_____

_____

2 $63 \div 9 \times (5 - 3) =$

3 Write an algebraic expression.

divide 16 by 8, then add 43

TUESDAY — Number Sense

1 Use rounding to estimate each value Then, add to estimate the sum.

$5.67 + $16.45

3 Complete the sentence using <, >, or =.

0.62 ☐ 8.9 − 6.0

2 Which digit is in the thousands place?

24 683 _____

4 Write the number in expanded form.

67 398 =

WEDNESDAY — Fractions and Decimals

1 Add.

$14 + \dfrac{3}{4} =$

2 Compare the quantities using <, >, or =.

$3\dfrac{1}{3}$ ▢ $\dfrac{12}{5}$

3 Write a fraction for each decimal.

a) 0.28

b) 1.67

c) 0.9

4 A recipe calls for half a tablespoon of sugar per serving. How many tablespoons of sugar do you need to make 8 servings? Draw a model to show your work.

THURSDAY — Geometry and Spatial Sense

1 Mark all the pairs of parallel sides in these shapes.

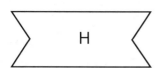

A B C D E F G H

2 Sort the shapes into the chart.

Category	Shapes
no parallel sides	
1 pair of parallel sides	
2 pairs of parallel sides	

Ray sorted the nails in his toolbox by length.

Nails Sorted by Length (in cm)

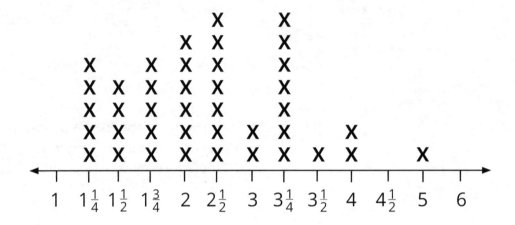

1 Ray found three more 4-cm nails and three $4\frac{1}{2}$-cm nails in the garage. He found another 2-cm nail in the bottom of a drawer. Add this data to the line plot.

2 How many nails does Ray have altogether? _____

3 Ray needs five 2-cm nails to hang pictures. Does he have enough? _____

4 Ray needs six $3\frac{1}{4}$-cm nails and six 5-cm nails to build a bookcase. Does he have enough? _____

If not, what does he need more of? _____

BRAIN STRETCH

Natalia needs a gift box with a volume of 240 cubic centimetres and a height of 8 centimetres. What are three possible combinations for the width and length of the box? Use whole numbers (no fractions or decimals).

MONDAY — Patterning and Algebra

1. Copy the patterns from Monday Question 1 on page 133.

a) ____, ____, ____, ____, ____

b) ____, ____, ____, ____, ____

2. Write the ordered pairs using a) for the *x*-coordinate and b) for the *y*-coordinate. The first pair has been done for you.

1ˢᵗ term (_1_ , _1_)

2ⁿᵈ term (____ , ____)

3ʳᵈ term (____ , ____)

4ᵗʰ term (____ , ____)

5ᵗʰ term (____ , ____)

3. Plot the ordered pairs on the coordinate plane and join the points. What do you see?

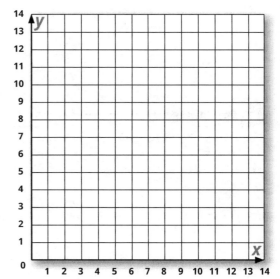

TUESDAY — Number Sense

1 6 ten thousands = _____ ones

2 Josh has $50 to spend at the store. He buys a video game for $38.65. What is his change?

3 Complete the sentence using <, >, or =.

0.8 [ ] 7.9 – 7.0

4 Make the greatest possible number with 2 decimal places using these digits.

7 9 4 8 7 6 2

1 Write the improper fraction as a mixed number.

$$\frac{13}{4}$$

2 Subtract. Show your work.

$$6 \frac{1}{2} - 3 \frac{4}{6}$$

3 Write a mixed number and improper fraction.

_____

4 On Thursday, $\frac{1}{6}$ of the students in the class were absent. If there are 36 students in total, how many students were absent? Draw a model to show your work.

THURSDAY — Geometry and Spatial Sense

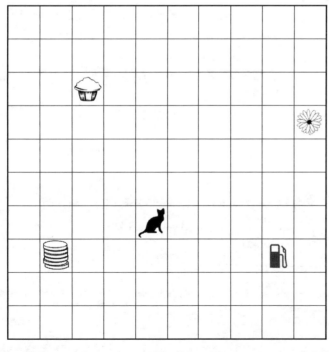

1 If you start at the ⛽ and go 5 blocks north and 6 blocks west. Where do you land?

2 Describe the route from the 🐱 to the 🧁

3 Describe your own route.

1 9 kg = _____ g

2 How many nickels are in $10?

3 George has a paper airplane that can fly 3.6 m. His friend Paul has one that can go 246 cm. Whose paper airplane can fly farther? How much farther can that person's airplane fly in centimetres?

4 Each cube has sides 1 metre. What is the total volume of the shape?

_____

BRAIN STRETCH

Ann Marie bought 2 bags of popcorn for $2.55 each and a drink for $1.20. She paid with $7.00. What are two combinations of coins that Ann Marie could receive as change? What is the fewest number of coins she could receive?

MONDAY — Patterning and Algebra

1 Write an algebraic expression.

take 40 away from 50, then multiply by 8

2 Evaluate the expression for $k = 9$.

a) $20 - k$

b) $30k$

3 How many times larger or smaller? Compare the expressions without calculating.

$2 \times (4 + 15)$ is _____ times

_____ than $4 \times (4 + 15)$

4 Carlos is 3 times as old as Eric. Eric is 30 years old. How old is Carlos?

TUESDAY — Number Sense

1 Round 34 983.3 to the nearest hundred.

2 Find the prime factorization of 27.

3 Round 13.25 to the nearest tenth.

4 Use rounding to estimate each value. Then, add to estimate the sum.

$4.13 + $2.89

5 Round to the nearest dime (10¢).

a) $0.43 _____   b) $0.36 _____

WEDNESDAY — Fractions and Decimals

1 Add, then simplify your answer.

$$\frac{4}{5} + \frac{3}{15} =$$

2 Is $\frac{5}{8}$ closest to 0, $\frac{1}{2}$, or 1?

3 Compare the fractions by writing <, >, or = in the box.

$$\frac{1}{2} \quad \boxed{} \quad \frac{3}{6}$$

4 Curtis's aunt is $3\frac{1}{2}$ times older than he is. If Curtis is 9, how old is his aunt?

THURSDAY — Geometry and Spatial Sense

1 Choose all the words that describe this shape.

A. rectangle

B. quadrilateral

C. rhombus

D. trapezoid

2 Classify the triangle by the lengths of its sides.

7 m, 7 m, 7 m

A.. isosceles

B. scalene

C. equilateral

3 Name and draw 2 special quadrilaterals.

4 Are these shapes congruent or similar?

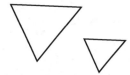

1 Which of the following units would be most appropriate to measure the weight of a pack of markers?

A. grams

B. milligrams

C. kilograms

2 Daryl drank 6 bottles of water each day for two weeks. Each bottle held 500 millilitres of water. How many litres of water did Daryl drink per week?

3 Calculate the perimeter and area of the polygon.

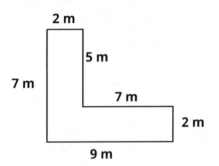

2 m

5 m

7 m

7 m

2 m

9 m

4 The volume of each box is 16 cubic metres. What is the volume of the whole 3D shape?

_____

BRAIN STRETCH

Pedram paid $30 for a new video game. He had $50 in savings. He says he spent $\frac{1}{4}$ of his savings on the video game. Is Pedram correct? Justify your answer. If Pedram is not correct, find the fraction of his savings he actually spent on the game.

Patterning and Algebra

1 a) Write the first five terms of each pattern.

Start at 4 and add 2 each time.

____, ____, ____, ____, ____

Start at 0 and add 2 each time.

____, ____, ____, ____, ____

b) Compare the two patterns. What do you notice?

_____

_____

2 Write an algebraic expression.

add 3 and 16, then multiply by 5

3 What is the missing number?

55, 65, _____ 85, 95

Number Sense

1 7 hundred thousands

= ____ ten thousands

2 How many dimes are in $20?

3 Estimate the difference by rounding each number to the nearest whole number, then subtracting.

9.27 − 6.94

4
$$\begin{array}{r} 4.4 \\ \times\, 1.6 \\ \hline \end{array}$$

WEDNESDAY   Fractions and Decimals

1 Write the improper fraction as a mixed number.

$$\frac{17}{12}$$

2 Subtract.

$$15\frac{1}{2} - 4 =$$

3 Order the fractions from least to greatest.

$$\frac{1}{2} \qquad \frac{3}{4} \qquad \frac{5}{8} \qquad \frac{1}{4}$$

4 Meghan went to the store with $5. She spent $\frac{1}{5}$ of her money on a fruit smoothie. How much did Meghan spend on the smoothie?

THURSDAY   Geometry and Spatial Sense

What are the coordinates of these places?

 Bakery _____

Bank _____

Flower shop _____

Gas station _____

Pet store _____

Restaurant _____

In the City

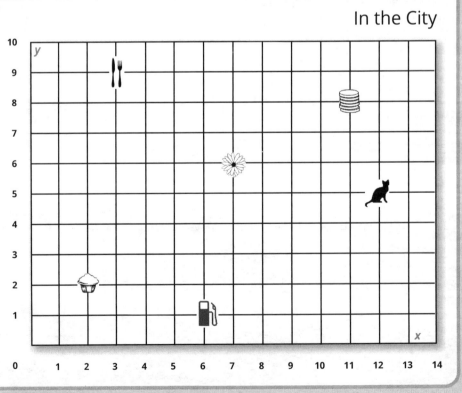

Measurement and Data

Mr. Brant's students sold cookies to raise money for a field trip.

Number of Boxes of Cookies Sold by Each Student

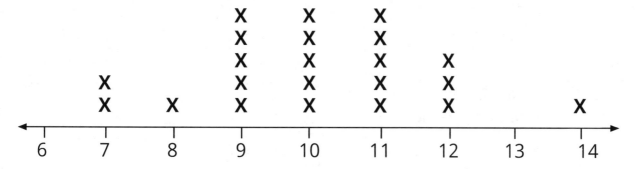

1 How many boxes of cookies did the students sell altogether? _____

2 If the class receives $2 for each box of cookies sold, how much money did the students raise? _____

3 Students who sell more than 10 boxes receive a prize from the cookie company. How many students in Mr. Brant's class received a prize? _____

BRAIN STRETCH

A garden is 8 metres longer than three times its width.
Let *w* represent the width of the garden and let *l* represent the length of the garden.

a) Write an expression for the length of the garden.

b) What an expression for the perimeter of the garden.

MONDAY Patterning and Algebra

1. Copy the patterns from Monday Question 1 on page 151.

a) ____, ____, ____, ____, ____

b) ____, ____, ____, ____, ____

2. Write the ordered pairs using a) for the *x*-coordinate and b) for the *y*-coordinate. The first pair has been done for you.

1st term (_4_ , _0_)

2nd term (___ , ___)

3rd term (___ , ___)

4th term (___ , ___)

5th term (___ , ___)

3. Plot the ordered pairs on the coordinate plane and join the points. What do you see?

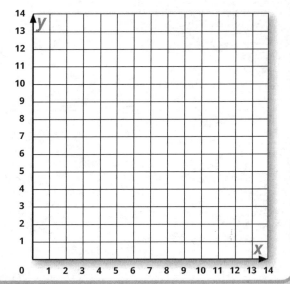

TUESDAY Number Sense

1 Round 56.98 to the nearest one.

2 Round to the nearest dollar ($1.00).

a) $2.40 _____ b) $1.72 _____

4
$$\begin{array}{r} 80 \\ \times\ 84 \\ \hline \end{array}$$

3
$$\begin{array}{r} 74.53 \\ -\ 13.06 \\ \hline \end{array}$$

1 Write the mixed number as an improper fraction.

$8\frac{10}{11}$

2 Add.

$10 + 2\frac{3}{7} =$

3 Is $\frac{1}{5}$ closest to 0, $\frac{1}{2}$, or 1?

4 A bag of flour that weighs $\frac{1}{2}$ kg is used to make 4 batches of bread. How much flour does each batch of bread use?

1 Choose all the words that describe this shape.

A. parallelogram
B. 4 sides
C. quadrilateral
D. rhombus

2 Name and draw a shape that has only one pair of parallel sides.

3 Classify the triangle.

A. isosceles
B. scalene
C. right
D. acute
E. obtuse

4 How many lines of symmetry are there?

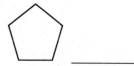

_____

1 6.7 litres = _____ millilitres

2 a) Find the length, width, and height of the rectangular prism. Each cube has sides 1 cm.

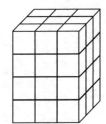

3 Write each time using the 24-hour clock.

a) 2 :00 P.M. _____

b) 7:15 A.M. _____

c) 11:35 P.M. _____

b) Use your answers in part a) to find the volume of the shape.

4 What is the volume of a pool that is 6 metres long, 2 metres wide, and 1 metre deep?

BRAIN STRETCH

Brendan made 7 pints of lemonade for a class party.
Carla made 8 more pints of lemonade for the class party.

a) How many cups of lemonade did Brendan and Carla make altogether?

b) If there are 20 students in the class, is there enough lemonade for each student to have 3 cups? Justify your answer.

Problem Solving Checklist

Understand the Problem

❑ Read the question carefully.
❑ Circle the key numbers.
❑ Underline the important information.
❑ Box any math action words.

Devise a Plan

❑ Choose a strategy to solve the problem.
❑ Choose the operation.
❑ Draw a model or diagram.

Solve the Problem

❑ Show all the steps in solving the problem.
❑ State your answer.
❑ Show the units.
❑ Check your calculations.
❑ Use math language to explain your thinking.

Review Your Thinking

❑ Does your answer make sense?

Problem Solving: Show Your Work

Multiplication Fact Fun

Multiply.

1. $0 \times 2 = $ _____

2. $5 \times 6 = $ _____

3. $8 \times 0 = $ _____

4. $8 \times 7 = $ _____

5. $9 \times 1 = $ _____

6. $1 \times 1 = $ _____

7. $2 \times 3 = $ _____

8. $9 \times 6 = $ _____

9. $8 \times 4 = $ _____

10. $5 \times 2 = $ _____

11. $6 \times 7 = $ _____

12. $8 \times 1 = $ _____

13. $7 \times 0 = $ _____

14. $5 \times 8 = $ _____

15. $2 \times 7 = $ _____

16. $6 \times 1 = $ _____

17. $0 \times 2 = $ _____

18. $8 \times 10 = $ _____

19. $8 \times 9 = $ _____

20. $3 \times 7 = $ _____

21. $4 \times 7 = $ _____

22. $4 \times 9 = $ _____

23. $10 \times 10 = $ _____

24. $10 \times 2 = $ _____

25. $3 \times 10 = $ _____

26. $2 \times 6 = $ _____

27. $1 \times 3 = $ _____

28. $4 \times 3 = $ _____

29. $8 \times 9 = $ _____

30. $5 \times 7 = $ _____

31. $4 \times 1 = $ _____

32. $8 \times 6 = $ _____

33. $8 \times 5 = $ _____

34. $5 \times 5 = $ _____

35. $6 \times 4 = $ _____

36. $3 \times 5 = $ _____

37. $4 \times 7 = $ _____

38. $9 \times 2 = $ _____

39. $9 \times 5 = $ _____

40. $4 \times 10 = $ _____

41. $1 \times 2 = $ _____

42. $8 \times 3 = $ _____

43. $7 \times 1 = $ _____

44. $2 \times 4 = $ _____

45. $4 \times 5 = $ _____

46. $3 \times 3 = $ _____

47. $7 \times 6 = $ _____

48. $6 \times 3 = $ _____

49. $8 \times 8 = $ _____

50. $4 \times 4 = $ _____

51. $2 \times 2 = $ _____

52. $0 \times 10 = $ _____

53. $3 \times 7 = $ _____

54. $7 \times 5 = $ _____

55. $9 \times 2 = $ _____

56. $5 \times 1 = $ _____

57. $1 \times 10 = $ _____

58. $10 \times 9 = $ _____

59. $9 \times 9 = $ _____

60. $6 \times 0 = $ _____

Multiplying by Multiples of 10, 100, 1000 and 10 000

Multiply

$7 \times 5000 =$ _____

7×5 ones = 35 ones = 35

7×5 tens = 35 tens = 350

7×5 hundreds = 35 hundreds = 3500

7×5 thousands = 35 thousands = 35 000

7×5 ten thousands = 350 thousands = 350 000

So $7 \times 5000 = 35\ 000$.

1. Use multiplication facts and patterns to help multiply.

a) $2 \times 3 =$ _____

$2 \times 30 =$ _____

$2 \times 300 =$ _____

$2 \times 3000 =$ _____

$2 \times 30\ 000 =$ _____

b) $4 \times 8 =$ _____

$4 \times 80 =$ _____

$4 \times 800 =$ _____

$4 \times 8000 =$ _____

$4 \times 80\ 000 =$ _____

c) $5 \times 1 =$ _____

$5 \times 10 =$ _____

$5 \times 100 =$ _____

$5 \times 1000 =$ _____

$5 \times 10\ 000 =$ _____

d) $8 \times 6 =$ _____

$8 \times 60 =$ _____

$8 \times 600 =$ _____

$8 \times 6000 =$ _____

$8 \times 60\ 000 =$ _____

e) $9 \times 5 =$ _____

$9 \times 50 =$ _____

$9 \times 500 =$ _____

$9 \times 5000 =$ _____

$9 \times 50\ 000 =$ _____

f) $3 \times 8 =$ _____

$3 \times 80 =$ _____

$3 \times 800 =$ _____

$3 \times 8000 =$ _____

$3 \times 80\ 000 =$ _____

g) $6 \times 7 =$ _____

$6 \times 70 =$ _____

$6 \times 700 =$ _____

$6 \times 7000 =$ _____

$6 \times 70\ 000 =$ _____

h) $3 \times 2 =$ _____

$3 \times 20 =$ _____

$3 \times 200 =$ _____

$3 \times 2000 =$ _____

$3 \times 20\ 000 =$ _____

i) $3 \times 5 =$ _____

$3 \times 50 =$ _____

$3 \times 500 =$ _____

$3 \times 5000 =$ _____

$3 \times 50\ 000 =$ _____

Multiplying by Multiples of 10, 100, 1000 and 10 000

Multiply.

1. $2 \times 70 =$ _____

2. $4 \times 200 =$ _____

3. $6 \times 5000 =$ _____

4. $1 \times 60\ 000 =$ _____

5. $40 \times 8 =$ _____

6. $10 \times 700 =$ _____

7. $3 \times 900 =$ _____

8. $5 \times 500 =$ _____

9. $7 \times 10\ 000 =$ _____

10. $9 \times 90 =$ _____

11. $2 \times 300 =$ _____

12. $4 \times 5000 =$ _____

13. $6 \times 40 =$ _____

14. $8 \times 800 =$ _____

15. $10 \times 9000 =$ _____

16. $1 \times 600 =$ _____

17. $3 \times 70 =$ _____

18. $5 \times 2000 =$ _____

19. $7 \times 30\ 000 =$ _____

20. $9 \times 700 =$ _____

21. $2 \times 4000 =$ _____

22. $6 \times 7000 =$ _____

23. $6 \times 80 =$ _____

24. $8 \times 2000 =$ _____

25. $10 \times 600 =$ _____

26. $2 \times 90 =$ _____

27. $9 \times 60\ 000 =$ _____

28. $3 \times 500 =$ _____

29. $8 \times 20 =$ _____

30. $1 \times 8000 =$ _____

31. $3 \times 200 =$ _____

32. $5 \times 50 =$ _____

33. $7 \times 40\ 000 =$ _____

34. $4 \times 1000 =$ _____

35. $2 \times 80 =$ _____

36. $4 \times 300 =$ _____

37. $4 \times 500 =$ _____

38. $8 \times 500 =$ _____

39. $10 \times 90 =$ _____

40. $5 \times 200 =$ _____

Number correct

_____
40

Multiplying Two-Digit Numbers by One-Digit Numbers

Step 1: Multiply the ones.

6 ones × 9 ones = 54 ones

Regroup 54 as 5 tens and 4 ones.

```
  5
  1 6
×   9
    4
```

Step 2: Multiply the tens.

1 ten × 9 ones = 9 tens

Then add the regrouped 5 tens.

9 tens + 5 tens = 14 tens

```
  5
  1 6
×   9
1 4 4
```

1 hundred + 4 tens + 4 ones

Multiply. **Hint:** Make sure to line up the numbers.

1.
```
  5 8
×   3
```

2.
```
  7 3
×   5
```

3.
```
  2 7
×   4
```

4.
```
  3 2
×   9
```

5.
```
  2 1
×   8
```

6.
```
  9 4
×   2
```

7.
```
  1 9
×   5
```

8.
```
  2 6
×   7
```

9.
```
  5 5
×   4
```

10.
```
  2 7
×   9
```

11.
```
  7 5
×   6
```

12.
```
  9 8
×   8
```

Multiplying Two-Digit Numbers by Two-Digit Numbers

Step 1: Multiply the ones.

6 ones × 9 ones = 54 ones

Regroup 54 as 5 tens and 4 ones.

```
    5
    1 6
  × 1 9
  _____
      4
```

Step 2: Multiply the tens.
1 ten × 9 ones = 9 tens
Then add the regrouped 5 tens.

9 tens + 5 tens = 14 tens

```
    5
    1 6
  × 1 9
  _____
  1 4 4
```

1 hundred + 4 tens + 4 ones

Step 3: Repeat steps 1 and 2 with the other tens. 1 ten × 6 ones = 6 tens. 1 ten × 1 ten = 1 hundred. Make sure to write the number in the right column!

Multiply. **Hint:** Make sure to line up the numbers.

1.
```
    5 8
  × 1 3
  _____

  _____
```

2.
```
    7 3
  × 4 5
  _____

  _____
```

3.
```
    2 7
  × 3 4
  _____

  _____
```

4.
```
    3 2
  × 2 9
  _____

  _____
```

5.
```
    2 1
  × 6 8
  _____

  _____
```

6.
```
    9 4
  × 2 2
  _____

  _____
```

7.
```
    1 9
  × 3 5
  _____

  _____
```

8.
```
    2 6
  × 1 7
  _____

  _____
```

9.
```
    5 5
  × 1 4
  _____

  _____
```

10.
```
    2 7
  × 9 9
  _____

  _____
```

11.
```
    7 5
  × 3 6
  _____

  _____
```

12.
```
    9 8
  × 2 8
  _____

  _____
```

Multiplying Multi-Digit Numbers by One-Digit Numbers

Step 1:
Multiply the ones.
6 ones × 5 ones
= 30 ones

Regroup 30 as
3 tens and 0 ones.

```
    ③
  3 1 6
×     5
─────────
      0
```

Step 2:
Multiply the tens.
1 ten × 5 ones
= 5 tens

Then add the
regrouped 3 tens.
5 tens + 3 tens
= 8 tens

```
    ③
  3 1 6
×     5
─────────
    8 0
```

Step 3:
Multiply the hundreds.
3 hundreds × 5 ones
= 15 hundreds

Regroup 1500 as
1 thousand and
5 hundreds.

```
    ③
  3 1 6
×     5
─────────
1 5 8 0
```

Since there are no
other thousands, write
the "1" in the answer.

Multiply. Regroup where necessary.

1.
```
  6 2 2
×     3
───────
```

2.
```
  2 1 9
×     8
───────
```

3.
```
  9 6 8
×     7
───────
```

4.
```
  8 1 3
×     6
───────
```

5.
```
  3 4 7
×     2
───────
```

6.
```
  4 9 1
×     5
───────
```

7.
```
  7 9 8
×     7
───────
```

8.
```
  1 8 5
×     4
───────
```

Multiply. Regroup where necessary.

9.
$$
\begin{array}{r}
726 \\
\times \quad 9 \\
\hline
\end{array}
$$

10.
$$
\begin{array}{r}
315 \\
\times \quad 5 \\
\hline
\end{array}
$$

11.
$$
\begin{array}{r}
245 \\
\times \quad 8 \\
\hline
\end{array}
$$

12.
$$
\begin{array}{r}
793 \\
\times \quad 2 \\
\hline
\end{array}
$$

13.
$$
\begin{array}{r}
555 \\
\times \quad 5 \\
\hline
\end{array}
$$

14.
$$
\begin{array}{r}
376 \\
\times \quad 7 \\
\hline
\end{array}
$$

15.
$$
\begin{array}{r}
721 \\
\times \quad 3 \\
\hline
\end{array}
$$

16.
$$
\begin{array}{r}
944 \\
\times \quad 4 \\
\hline
\end{array}
$$

17.
$$
\begin{array}{r}
855 \\
\times \quad 2 \\
\hline
\end{array}
$$

18.
$$
\begin{array}{r}
347 \\
\times \quad 3 \\
\hline
\end{array}
$$

19.
$$
\begin{array}{r}
652 \\
\times \quad 4 \\
\hline
\end{array}
$$

20.
$$
\begin{array}{r}
193 \\
\times \quad 6 \\
\hline
\end{array}
$$

21.
$$
\begin{array}{r}
4467 \\
\times \quad 3 \\
\hline
\end{array}
$$

22.
$$
\begin{array}{r}
6159 \\
\times \quad 9 \\
\hline
\end{array}
$$

23.
$$
\begin{array}{r}
2728 \\
\times \quad 5 \\
\hline
\end{array}
$$

24.
$$
\begin{array}{r}
9271 \\
\times \quad 4 \\
\hline
\end{array}
$$

25.
$$
\begin{array}{r}
5248 \\
\times \quad 8 \\
\hline
\end{array}
$$

26.
$$
\begin{array}{r}
3521 \\
\times \quad 7 \\
\hline
\end{array}
$$

27.
$$
\begin{array}{r}
2319 \\
\times \quad 6 \\
\hline
\end{array}
$$

28.
$$
\begin{array}{r}
7216 \\
\times \quad 8 \\
\hline
\end{array}
$$

Estimating a Product

To estimate, round at least one factor to make it easier to multiply. The factors are the numbers you multiply together.

Rounding one factor:
Estimate: 7 × 91   Round 91 to 100.

Think: For 7 × 100, you know that 7 × 10 = 70.
Add one zero to multiply by 100.
The estimated product is 7 × 100 = 700.

1. Estimate by rounding one factor. Show your work.
   Hint: Round to the nearest ten or the nearest hundred.

a) 70 × 57

b) 9 × 44

c) 7 × 316

d) 5 × 85

e) 10 × 32

f) 60 × 65

g) 11 × 28

h) 4 × 79

i) 30 × 93

Estimating a Product

Rounding both factors:
Estimate: 32 × 67   Round both factors. 32 is close to 30 and 67 is close to 70.

Think: For 30 × 70, you know that 3 × 7 = 21.
Add the zeros from 30 and 70.
The estimated product is 30 × 70 = 2100.

2. Estimate by rounding both factors. Show your work.
   Hint: Round to the nearest ten or the nearest hundred.

a) 34 × 29

b) 67 × 63

c) 83 × 87

d) 81 × 39

e) 26 × 31

f) 98 × 18

g) 53 × 546

h) 12 × 110

i) 36 × 791

Division Fact Fun

Divide.

1. $36 \div 6 =$ _____
2. $12 \div 6 =$ _____
3. $48 \div 8 =$ _____
4. $30 \div 3 =$ _____
5. $7 \div 0 =$ _____
6. $21 \div 3 =$ _____
7. $54 \div 9 =$ _____
8. $28 \div 7 =$ _____
9. $15 \div 5 =$ _____
10. $35 \div 5 =$ _____
11. $63 \div 9 =$ _____
12. $16 \div 8 =$ _____
13. $6 \div 2 =$ _____
14. $20 \div 2 =$ _____
15. $30 \div 3 =$ _____
16. $100 \div 10 =$ _____
17. $28 \div 4 =$ _____
18. $24 \div 4 =$ _____
19. $27 \div 9 =$ _____
20. $6 \div 1 =$ _____

21. $27 \div 9 =$ _____
22. $40 \div 5 =$ _____
23. $12 \div 2 =$ _____
24. $90 \div 10 =$ _____
25. $24 \div 3 =$ _____
26. $4 \div 4 =$ _____
27. $8 \div 8 =$ _____
28. $28 \div 4 =$ _____
29. $10 \div 0 =$ _____
30. $6 \div 3 =$ _____
31. $63 \div 9 =$ _____
32. $42 \div 7 =$ _____
33. $35 \div 7 =$ _____
34. $18 \div 2 =$ _____
35. $9 \div 0 =$ _____
36. $70 \div 10 =$ _____
37. $36 \div 9 =$ _____
38. $50 \div 10 =$ _____
39. $56 \div 7 =$ _____
40. $14 \div 7 =$ _____

41. $16 \div 2 =$ _____
42. $72 \div 9 =$ _____
43. $49 \div 7 =$ _____
44. $30 \div 6 =$ _____
45. $54 \div 9 =$ _____
46. $14 \div 2 =$ _____
47. $64 \div 8 =$ _____
48. $81 \div 9 =$ _____
49. $8 \div 1 =$ _____
50. $9 \div 1 =$ _____
51. $18 \div 9 =$ _____
52. $9 \div 3 =$ _____
53. $12 \div 3 =$ _____
54. $60 \div 6 =$ _____
55. $0 \div 1 =$ _____
56. $3 \div 0 =$ _____
57. $40 \div 10 =$ _____
58. $2 \div 1 =$ _____
59. $32 \div 4 =$ _____
60. $72 \div 8 =$ _____

Dividing Multiples of 10, 100, 1000, and 10 000

Divide: $4000 \div 8 =$

Think: 40 ones $\div 8 = \underline{5}$ ones $= \underline{5}$

40 tens $\div 8 = \underline{5}$ tens $= \underline{50}$

40 hundreds $\div 8 = \underline{5}$ hundreds $= \underline{500}$

So $4000 \div 8 = \underline{500}$.

1. Use division facts and patterns to help you divide.

a) $6 \div 3 =$ _____ $60 \div 3 =$ _____ $600 \div 3 =$ _____ $6000 \div 3 =$ _____ $60\ 000 \div 3 =$ _____	**b)** $18 \div 3 =$ _____ $180 \div 3 =$ _____ $1800 \div 3 =$ _____ $18\ 000 \div 3 =$ _____ $180\ 000 \div 3 =$ _____	**c)** $5 \div 5 =$ _____ $50 \div 5 =$ _____ $500 \div 5 =$ _____ $5000 \div 5 =$ _____ $50\ 000 \div 5 =$ _____
d) $9 \div 9 =$ _____ $90 \div 9 =$ _____ $900 \div 9 =$ _____ $9000 \div 9 =$ _____ $90\ 000 \div 9 =$ _____	**e)** $10 \div 2 =$ _____ $100 \div 2 =$ _____ $1000 \div 2 =$ _____ $10\ 000 \div 2 =$ _____ $100\ 000 \div 2 =$ _____	**f)** $35 \div 5 =$ _____ $350 \div 5 =$ _____ $3500 \div 5 =$ _____ $35\ 000 \div 5 =$ _____ $350\ 000 \div 5 =$ _____

Dividing Multiples of 10, 100, 1000, and 10 000

1. $80 \div 8 =$ _____

2. $1800 \div 10 =$ _____

3. $3000 \div 2 =$ _____

4. $400 \div 2 =$ _____

5. $1200 \div 12 =$ _____

6. $240 \div 4 =$ _____

7. $560 \div 8 =$ _____

8. $9600 \div 8 =$ _____

9. $70\,000 \div 10 =$ _____

10. $100 \div 100 =$ _____

11. $11\,000 \div 11 =$ _____

12. $7200 \div 12 =$ _____

13. $350 \div 5 =$ _____

14. $600 \div 60 =$ _____

15. $840 \div 7 =$ _____

16. $80 \div 10 =$ _____

17. $6300 \div 9 =$ _____

18. $500 \div 5 =$ _____

19. $990 \div 11 =$ _____

20. $4800 \div 8 =$ _____

21. $100 \div 20 =$ _____

22. $1200 \div 3 =$ _____

23. $48\,000 \div 8 =$ _____

24. $5600 \div 7 =$ _____

25. $900 \div 9 =$ _____

26. $72 \div 8 =$ _____

27. $90 \div 9 =$ _____

28. $25\,000 \div 25 =$ _____

29. $350 \div 5 =$ _____

30. $48\,000 \div 4 =$ _____

31. $99\,000 \div 9 =$ _____

32. $880 \div 8 =$ _____

33. $2400 \div 6 =$ _____

34. $6000 \div 2 =$ _____

35. $140 \div 7 =$ _____

36. $250 \div 5 =$ _____

37. $360\,000 \div 9 =$ _____

38. $60 \div 12 =$ _____

39. $30 \div 6 =$ _____

40. $150 \div 5 =$ _____

Number correct

_____
40

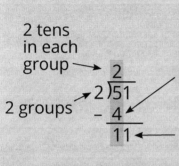

Step 1: Divide to find how many tens can go in each group.

Step 2: Multiply: 4 tens are placed. Subtract: 1 ten is left.
So, 1 ten and 1 one are left. Write 1 beside the 1 ten.

Step 3: Divide to find how many ones can go in each group.

Step 4: Multiply: 10 ones are placed. Subtract to find that 1 one is left. So, the answer is 25 R 1.

$$\begin{array}{r} 25 \leftarrow \text{5 ones in each group} \\ 2\overline{)51} \\ -\ 4 \\ \hline 11 \\ -\ 10 \\ \hline 1 \end{array}$$

R means remainder.

Find the quotient. **Hint:** The answer in division is called the **quotient**.

1. $5\overline{)35}$

2. $2\overline{)62}$

3. $2\overline{)78}$

4. $3\overline{)11}$

5. $4\overline{)53}$

6. $6\overline{)48}$

7. $2\overline{)79}$

8. $5\overline{)16}$

9. $4\overline{)70}$

10. $5\overline{)88}$

11. $6\overline{)89}$

12. $3\overline{)38}$

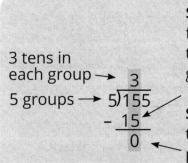

3 tens in each group →
5 groups → 5)155
−15
0

Step 1: Divide to find how many tens can go in each group.

Step 2: Multiply: 1 ten and 5 ones are placed. Subtract: there is nothing left. So, write 3 above the number.

1 one in each group

31
5)155
−15↓
05
−5
0

bring down to complete division

Step 3: Divide to find how many ones can go in each group.

Step 4: Multiply: 1 one is placed. Subtract: there is nothing left. So, the answer is 31.

Find the quotient. **Hint:** The answer in division is called the **quotient**.

1. 5)605

2. 2)366

3. 2)900

4. 3)933

5. 4)155

6. 6)119

7. 2)809

8. 5)361

9. 4)467

10. 5)225

11. 6)391

12. 3)923

Divide.

$$\begin{array}{r} 7\,8 \\ 4\,)\overline{3\,1\,2} \\ -\,2\,8 \\ \hline 3\,2 \\ -\,3\,2 \\ \hline 0 \end{array}$$

Hint: There are fewer hundreds than groups. So, the division starts with the tens.

1. $2)\overline{6\,4\,2}$

2. $5)\overline{5\,3\,0}$

3. $3)\overline{9\,9\,9}$

4. $2)\overline{1\,9\,4}$

5. $4)\overline{7\,2\,4}$

6. $2)\overline{3\,7\,0}$

7. $2)\overline{6\,1\,6}$

8. $5)\overline{9\,1\,5}$

9. $4)\overline{3\,0\,4}$

10. $6)\overline{1\,3\,8}$

11. $3)\overline{1\,4\,7}$

All quadrilaterals have 4 sides but some quadrilaterals are special.

A **parallelogram** is a quadrilateral with 2 pairs of parallel sides.

Double and single tick marks indicate sides of equal length.

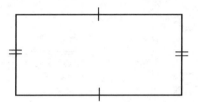

Parallel lines are straight lines that stay the same distance apart. They never meet.

Arrows indicate the lines are parallel.

Some parallelograms have **right angles**. A right angle makes a square corner.

A small square symbol in the corner indicates a right angle.

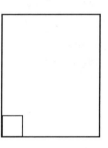

A **rectangle** is a parallelogram with 2 pairs of parallel sides and 4 right angles.

A **square** is a parallelogram with 4 equal sides and 4 right angles.

A **rhombus** is a parallelogram with 4 equal sides but no right angles.

3D Figures

3D Figure	Number of Faces	Shape of Faces	Number of Edges	Number of Vertices
Sphere	0	none	0	0
Cube	6	square	12	8
Square-based Pyramid	5	4 triangles, 1 square	8	5
Cone	1	circle	0	0
Cylinder	2	circles	0	0
Rectangular Prism	6	rectangles	12	8

Congruent and Similar Shapes

Figures that have the same exact size and shape are called congruent.

Figures can be congruent even though they are not in the same position.

Figures are similar when the only difference is size.

Figures can be similar even though they are not in the same position.

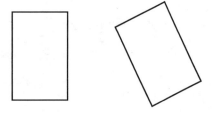

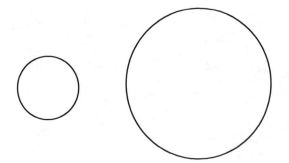

Classifying Angles

A right angle is 90°.	An acute angle is less than 90°.	An obtuse angle is greater than 90°.	A straight angle is 180°.
90°	40°	120°	180°

Units of Measurement

	Bigger ⬅			Base Unit	Smaller ➡		
Length	Kilometre km	Hectometre (hm)	Decametre (dam)	Metre (m)	Decimetre (dm)	Centimetre (cm)	Millimetre (mm)
Weight	Kilogram (kg)	Hectogram (hg)	Decagram (dag)	Gram (g)	Decigram (dg)	Centigram (cg)	Milligram (mg)
Volume	Kilolitre (kL)	Hectolitre (hL)	Decalitre (daL)	Litre (L)	Decilitre (dL)	Centilitre (cL)	Millilitre (mL)
How many are in 1 metre/ gram/litre?	.001	.01	.1	1	10	100	1000
How many metres/ grams/litres are in this?	1000	100	10	1	.1	.01	.001

Displaying Data

BAR GRAPHS

Bar graphs use horizontal or vertical bars that display data.

- Bar graphs are a good way to display data you want to compare.

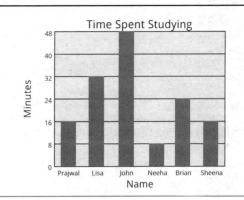

LINE GRAPHS

Line graphs use points that are joined and that represent data over time.

- Line graphs are a good way to display data that shows change over time.

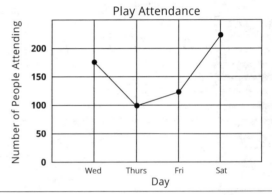

CIRCLE OR PIE GRAPHS

These are graphs in which circles are used to represent a whole and are divided into parts that represent parts of the whole.

- Circle or pie graphs are a good way to display data if you want to compare parts of a whole.

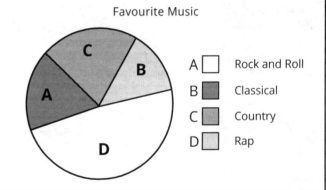

PICTOGRAPHS

Pictographs use pictures or icons to show data and to compare information. Each picture or icon can represent more than one object. A key is used to show what each picture represents.

- Pictographs are a good way to display data you want to compare.

Conducting a Survey

SURVEY	A method of collecting a sample of data by asking people questions
SAMPLE	A section of a whole group
FREQUENCY	The number of times an answer is chosen
DATA	A collection of information usually gathered by observation, questioning, or measurement

❏ **Plan a survey question.**

Think of a clear survey question that provides for all possibilities. This is my survey question...

_____

_____

❏ **Decide on a sample of data.**

Make certain the survey results are not biased by surveying people who are typical of the group of people you are interested in, such as grade 5 girls and boys. Think about how many people you will ask to take part in the survey. For my survey, I am going to ask....

_____

_____

❏ **Conduct the survey.**

On a separate piece of paper, record people's responses to the survey. Use a tally mark to record each response.

❏ **Organize the data into a data table.**

After completing the survey, count the tallies for each response and record the frequency in a data table.

❏ **Graph the data.**

Choose a type of graph to display the data.

I will display the data from the survey using a_____ graph because

_____

_____

❏ **Write about the results.**

On a separate piece of paper, write about what you infer from your graph.

Math Glossary

* **Words** = problem solving words

A

Above: In or at a place that is higher.

Acute: An angle that measures less than 90°.

Acute Triangle: A triangle with three acute angles.

Addend: Any number used to add to get a sum. In 7 + 2 = 9, the addends are 7 and 2.

Addition: An operation where two or more numbers are combined.

Algebra: An area of math where numbers are represented by letters.

Algebraic Expression: A mathematical phrase that can have numbers, letters, and operation signs. It does not have an equal sign.

Algorithm: A set of steps to follow for carrying out a calculation.

Always: At all times.

Amount: A quantity, number of, total, sum, or size

Analogue Clock: A tool used to show the time. It has moving hands and hours marked from 1 to 12.

Angle: The figure formed when two lines meet at a vertex.

Approximately: to come close to or be nearly the same as.

Area: The space a surface takes up. Area is measured in square units.

Array: Numbers or objects arranged in rows and columns.

Attribute: A characteristic that describes something. Colour and size are examples.

Axis: Real or imaginary reference line. *X*-axis: the horizontal axis of a graph. *Y*-axis: the vertical axis of a graph.

B

Bar Graph: A graph that uses horizontal or vertical bars to show data.

Base Ten: A number system based on ten.

Behind: At the back or rear.

Below: In or at a place that is lower than another object.

Benchmark: A standard by which something can be measured. A reference to help judge something.

Beside: At the side of or next to.

Between: In a space that separates objects or times.

Broken Line Graph: A graph that uses points to show data. The points are sometimes connected with a line.

Math Glossary

*Words** = problem solving words

C

Calculate: To figure out by computation.

Cardinal Direction: The main points of a compass—north, east, south, and west.

Cartesian Plane: A plane containing two perpendicular axes (*x* and *y*).

Capacity: The amount a container can hold.

Celsius: A temperature measurement scale used in the metric system. For example 0° is the temperature of freezing water.

Centimetre: A metric unit used for measuring length. 100 cm = 1 m

Century: A period of time equal to 100 years.

Certain: An event that will definitely happen.

Chance: The likelihood that a particular outcome will happen.

Circle Graph: A graph that uses a circle divided into sectors to represent data. Also called a pie chart.

Circumference: The distance around a circle. Circumference = 2 × 3.14 × radius, or C = 2πr.

Classify: To arrange and order.

Clock: A tool that measures and shows time.

Collect: To bring together.

Compare: To find what is the same and what is different about numbers or objects.

Conclusion: The result or outcome of an act or process.

Constant: A number that does not change.

Coordinates: The values in an ordered pair that can be shown on a coordinate grid.

Coordinate Systems: An ordered pair of numbers that show location.

Concrete Graph: A graph where real objects are used to represent data.

Congruent: Having the same shape and size.

Coin: A piece of metal used as money.

D

Data: A collection of information that is often shown on tables or graphs.

Decade: A period of time equal to 10 years.

Decimal Point: The point which separates the integer and fraction parts of a number.

Decimal System: A number system that is based on 10. Also called the base 10 system.

Decomposition: A way to separate a number into parts.

Decrease: To get smaller.

* **Define:** State the meaning of something.

* **Words** = problem solving words

Degree: A unit for measuring the size of angles. For example 60°

Denominator: The number of parts that a whole is divided into. It is the bottom number of a fraction.

* Describe: Express an idea using words, numbers, and pictures.

* Determine: To find out exactly.

Diagram: A drawing that represents something.

Diameter: A straight line passing through the centre of a circle touching two points on the edge of the circumference.

Difference: The result of subtraction.

Digit: A symbol used to make a number. 0, 1, 2, 3, 4, 5, 6, 7, 8, and 9 are the digits we use to make numbers such as 12.

Dime: A Canadian or an American coin valued at 10 cents.

Discrete Data: Data that has a certain number of possible values.

Distance: The length between points.

Division: An operation where a quantity is grouped into equal parts. See <u>multiplication</u> for definition.

Double: Twice as much.

E

Edge: Where two faces of a 3D object meet.

Elapsed Time: The measured duration of an event.

Equal: Having the same value.

Equality: The state of being equal.

Equation: A mathematical sentence that uses an equal sign that shows two expressions are equal.

Equilateral: Having all sides or faces equal.

Equivalent Fractions: Fractions that have the same value but may have different numerators and denominators.

Estimate: To approximate an answer. Rounding is an example.

Even Number: A number that can be divided evenly by two.

Event: Possible outcome(s) in an experiment.

Expanded Form: A way of writing numbers that shows the value of each digit. An example is 200 + 40 + 1.

Experiment: A test to discover something unknown, or to verify something expected.

* Explain: To offer reasons and/or to justify.

Expression: One or a group of mathematical symbols representing a number or quantity.

Math Glossary

Words = problem solving words

F

Face: One surface of a 3D object.

Factors: Numbers that are multiplied to produce a product.

Fair: When events are equally likely.

Favourable Outcome: Positive results.

Few: A small number.

Flip: To turn over.

Fraction: A number that represents part of a group or a whole.

Frequency: The number of times an event occurs.

G

Graph: A drawing or diagram used to record information.

Greater Than: More than.

Grouping: Dividing things into equal groups or sets.

Growing Pattern: A pattern in which the terms become larger.

H

Height: A measurement from top to bottom.

Horizontal: Parallel to the horizon.

Hour: A unit of time that is equal to 60 minutes.

I

* Investigate: To explore or research by problem solving.

Impossible: An event that cannot happen.

Improper Fraction: A fraction whose numerator is larger than the denominator.

Increase: To get larger.

Inequality: Not equal in size, amount or value.

Interpret: To translate or analyze.

Intersecting Lines: Two lines that cross.

Math Glossary

* **Words** = problem solving words

Interval: The distance between two points.

Inverse Operations: Two operations that are opposite. Addition is the opposite of subtraction.
$2 + 3 = 5$ $5 - 2 = 3$

Isosceles: A triangle with two equal sides and two angles the same size.

J

* **Justify:** To support or defend.

K

Kilogram: A metric unit for measuring mass (weight). 1 kilogram (kg) = 1000 grams (g)

Kilometre: A metric unit for measuring distance (km). 1 kilometre (km) = 1000 metres (m)

L

Least: The smallest number in a group or a set of data.

Length: The measurement of distance between two points.

Less: Not as many as another number.

Likelihood: A chance that an outcome will happen.

Likely: An event that is expected to happen more than half the time.

Line: A length (straight or curved) without breadth or thickness.

* **List:** To itemize or tally.

Litre: A metric unit of capacity.

Location: The place or position of an object.

M

Many: Opposite of few.

Mass: The quantity of matter in an object often measured in grams or kilograms.

Mean: The sum of a set of values divided by the number of values in the set. It is also referred to as average.

Measure: Using standard units to find a size or a quantity.

Median: The middle value in an ordered set of values. The values are lined up in order from the smallest to the largest to find the middle value.

Math Glossary

Metre: A metric unit used for measuring length.

Metric System: A decimal system of measurement using multiples of ten.

Millennium: A period of time equal to 1000 years.

Millimetre: A metric unit for measuring length. 10 mm = 1 cm

Mixed Number: A number written as a whole number and a fraction.

Mode: The most frequently occurring value in a set of values.

More likely: An event that will probably occur.

More: The greater amount.

Most: The greatest amount.

Multiplication: An operation where a number is added to itself a number of times.

N

Net: A flat shape that can be folded into a 3D object.

Never: Absolutely not. The probability is zero.

Nickel: A Canadian or an American coin valued at 5 cents.

Non standard: Objects such as paper clips used as measurement units.

Numerator: The number above the line in a fraction.

O

Obtuse Angle: Any angle between 90° and 180°.

Obtuse Triangle: A triangle with one obtuse angle.

Odd Number: A number that cannot be divided evenly by two.

Operation: In math, there are four operations to solve problems: addition, subtraction, multiplication, and division.

Ordered Pair: A pair of numbers used to locate a point on a coordinate grid. An example is (9, 12).

Ordinal Number: A number that shows a place or position.

Outcome: The different ways that an event can happen in a probability experiment.

P

Parallel: Lines that are the same distance apart and never meet.

Parallelogram: A quadrilateral where the opposite sides are parallel and equal in length.

Pattern: An arrangement of shapes, numbers, or objects that repeat.

Math Glossary

* Words = problem solving words

Penny: An American coin valued at 1 cent.

Pentagon: A polygon with five sides.

Perimeter: The distance around a shape or an object.

Pictograph: A graph that shows data using pictures.

Place Value: The value of a digit depending on its position in a number.

Polyhedron: Three dimensional figures with plane faces.

Polygon: A closed shape having three or more sides.

* Predict: Describe what may happen based on the information provided in the question.

Primary Data: Data observed or collected directly from first-hand knowledge.

Prime Number: A whole number that has only two factors. It can be divided evenly only by one and itself. (2, 3, 5, 7, and 11 are some examples)

Prism: A 3D object with two bases that are parallel and congruent.

Probability: The chance or likelihood of something happening.

Probably: An event that might occur.

Product: The answer when two numbers are multiplied. The product of 2 and 4 is 8.

Pyramid: A 3D object with a polygon as a base and triangular faces that taper to the same vertex.

Q

Quadrant: Any quarter of a plane divided by an *x* and *y* axis.

Quadrilateral: A polygon having four sides.

Quantity: Amount of something.

Quarter: A Canadian or an American coin valued at 25 cents.

Quotient: The answer after dividing one number by another one. For example, the quotient of 6 ÷ 2 is 3.

R

Range: The difference of the highest number and lowest number in a set of data.

Ray: A line that has a starting point but no endpoint.

Ratio: A comparative value of two or more amount. An example is 2:4 or as a fraction.

Reasoning: Evidence or arguments used in thinking or forming conclusions.

Reciprocal: One of two numbers whose products are 1.

Rectangle: A quadrilateral with four right angles and two pairs of opposite equal parallel sides. Length and width can be either equal or unequal.

Rectangular Prism: A prism with rectangular faces.

Math Glossary

* **Words** = problem solving words

Reflection: A mirror image of a shape or an object.

Remainder: The amount left over after dividing a number.

Represent: To show.

Rhombus: A type of quadrilateral, a parallelogram with four equal sides and opposite angles.

Right Angle: An angle which is equal to 90°.

Right Angled Triangle: A triangle with one angle measuring 90°.

Rotation: A circular movement where a central point is fixed and everything else moves around that point.

Rotational Symmetry: The shape or image is rotated and still looks the same. This image can be rotated to three different positions and it would always look the same.

Round: To change a number to a more convenient number. For example, 22 rounded to the nearest 10 is 20.

S

Scalene: A triangle with all three sides in different lengths.

Secondary Data: Data collected by someone other than the user.

Set: A collection of items.

Sequence: An ordered set of numbers, shapes, or other mathematical objects that are arranged according to a rule.

* Show Your Work: Use pictures, words, numbers, diagrams, symbols, and graphs to show your thinking as you arrived at your solution.

Side: One of the lines that make up a 2D shape.

Simplify: To reduce the numerator and denominator in a fraction or to the smallest numbers possible.

Skeleton: An outline or sketch.

Skip Count: Counting forward or backward using a specific multiple or interval.

Slide: To move an item in direction without rotating it.

Sort: To organize according to shape, colour, or number.

Square-Based Pyramid: A pyramid with a square base.

Square: A quadrilateral with four equal sides, four right angles, four lines of symmetry, and the opposite sides are parallel.

Standard: Using a measurement unit as a means for measure.

Stem and Leaf Plot: A data display where groups of data are arranged by place value.

* Strategy: A plan, or way to solve a problem or get to an answer.

Subtraction: An operation where one number is taken away from another number.

Sum: The result of addition.

Surface area: Total area of a surface of a 3D figure and is measured in square units.

Math Glossary

* Words = problem solving words

Survey: A method of collecting data.

Symmetry: An object has symmetry if one half of the object is a mirror image of the other half.

T

Table: An organizer that shows data in rows and columns.

Tally: Using marks to record counts or votes.

Tangram: An ancient Chinese puzzle based on a square cut into seven pieces.

Temperature: A measurement of how hot or cold something is.

Tenth: One part of ten equal parts.

Term: One of the numbers in a sequence or series of numbers.

Three-Dimensional Object: A figure that has height, depth, and width. Written as 3D.

Time: Time is the ongoing sequence of events taking place. Time is measured using clocks and other timing devices.

Transformation: A change in position or size.

Translation: Also called a slide, moves every point on a shape in the same direction and distance.

Triangular Prism: A polyhedron, a prism with two identical triangular bases.

Turn: To rotate.

Two-Dimensional Shapes: A shape that has only width and height and no thickness. Written as 2D.

U

Unit: Another name for one.

Unlikely: An event that is expected to happen less than half the time.

V

Value: A numerical amount.

Variable: A quantity that can change. It is a symbol for a number that has not yet been determined. An example is *x*.

Venn diagram: A diagram using circles or other shapes showing relationships among sets of data.

Vertex: An example is x in 2D geometry, where two lines meet. In 3D geometry, where three or more edges meet. The plural of vertex is vertices.

Vertical: In an up-down position.

Volume: The amount of space an object occupies. Volume is measured in cubic units.

Math Glossary

*Words = problem solving words

W

Weight: The measure of how heavy something is.

Whole Number: Any number used for counting including zero.

Width: The distance across from one side to the other.

X

***x*-axis:** The horizontal axis of a graph.

***x*-coordinate:** The position of a point along the *x*-axis. The *x*-coordinate is written first in an ordered pair of coordinates (*x,y*).

Y

***y*-axis:** The vertical axis of a graph.

***y*-coordinate:** The position of a point along the *y*-axis. The *y*-coordinate is written second in an ordered pair of coordinates (*x,y*).

Answers

Earthquakes, pp. 26–27

1. Huge slabs of rock under Earth's surface.

2. Students should complete the chart as follows

Cause	Effect
Two tectonic plates get stuck as they rub against each other.	Force builds up as the plates keep trying to move.
There is enough force to make the plates move again.	The plates move quickly for a few moments.
The plates move quickly for a few moments.	This movement causes the surface of Earth to tremble and shake.
An earthquake is so weak that people do not notice it.	There is no damage.
A powerful earthquake causes the ground to shake a lot.	There is a lot of damage to buildings and other structures.

3. People have put in place rules for building new structures strong enough to stand up to most earthquakes.

4. Many older structures were built before rules were put in place to make buildings strong enough to stand up to earthquakes.

A Truly Canadian Animal, pp. 28–29

1. The main idea of this text is that the beaver is a truly Canadian animal that has changed Canada in a number of ways.

2. The beaver changed Canada's history by attracting Europeans to the country because they wanted its fur, and causing Europeans to settle in the country because they had work through the fur trade. The beaver is changing Canada's environment by building dams that change how streams flow and that form ponds and marshes that other animals depend on.

3. Answers will vary. Ensure that students write five sentences.

4. Answers will vary. Ensure that students provide a good explanation for their choice.

How Does That Fly? pp. 30–31

1. Gravity wants to pull the plane down to Earth. Drag wants to pull the plane backward. Lift and thrust overcome these two forces so a plane can fly.

2. The diagram relates to the part on weight, lift, drag, and thrust. It helped me understand the information better because it shows which forces act against each other and the direction the forces act in. It summarizes what the writing says.

3. When an airplane is flying straight and level, weight is equal to lift, and drag is equal to thrust.

4. It means to use the smallest amount of fuel to get somewhere. Planes have become more fuel efficient, meaning that they use less fuel than they used to use to fly the same distances.

5. Jet engines are more powerful so the planes can fly faster. The faster they fly, the more lift they have. So planes can be bigger and still fly.

6. The differences between the first passenger planes and airplanes today is that planes can now carry more passengers, are much bigger, can fly farther, are built lighter, and have jet engines that are more powerful.

The Legacy of Terry Fox, pp. 32–33

1. Terry's legacy is the Terry Fox Run that is held every year to raise money for cancer research.

2. *Amputated* means to cut off a part of the body such as a leg. Terry had an artificial leg after the operation, so the doctors must have cut off his leg. An *amputee* is a person who has had an amputation. Both words are about the same thing, but *amputated* is doing something (verb) and *amputee* is a person (noun).

3. He read about an amputee that ran a marathon in New York. He felt sorry for other people in the hospital who had cancer, especially the children, and wanted to help them.

4. The Terry Fox Run in Canada happens every year on the second Sunday after Labour Day. International Terry Fox Runs can happen any day. The Terry Fox Run in Canada raises money for cancer research in Canada. International Terry Fox Runs usually raise money for cancer research in the country they take place in.

5. Terry Fox cared about other people. He wanted to help people who had cancer. He was very determined. He trained hard so he could run with his artificial leg. Even when he had cancer again, he wanted to help by planning to raise more money through yearly runs. He never gave up. He ran for 143 days before he finally had to stop because he was sick again.

The Teacher and the Thief, pp. 34–35

1. Benzei does keep his promise to do everything possible to help each one of his students learn. He says that if he doesn't teach Taku, no one will, so that's why he doesn't expel him for stealing.

2. Things started to go missing shortly after Taku came to the school.

3. The student is no longer allowed to attend the school.
4. The clue is that the man who spoke up to defend Benzei said that Benzei must have a reason for not expelling Taku.
5. The students probably believed that if Benzei cared enough to keep a student who steals, then he cared more about all his students than other teachers would.
6. Answers may vary. Students might suggest that Benzei could have talked to Taku to convince him to stop stealing, or Benzei could have punished Taku in some way other than by expelling him.

Avoiding Sentence Fragments, p. 38
1. Circle the following **a)** complete subject **b)** complete predicate **c)** both are missing **d)** complete predicate **e)** both are missing **f)** complete subject
2. a) CS **b)** SF **c)** CS **d)** SF **e)** SF **f)** SF **g)** CS

Combining Sentences, p. 39
1. a) I was tired, so I went to bed. **b)** Kim might win the race, or she might come in second. **c)** I can help you, or you could ask Jeff for help. **d)** The sun was shining, so I put on sunscreen. **e)** Is Travis coming, or is he still sick? **f)** The bus was coming, so I ran to the bus stop.

Correcting Run-On Sentences, pp. 40–41
1. a) check mark **b)** RO **c)** RO **d)** check mark **e)** RO **f)** RO
2. a) I forgot umbrella. I got wet in the rain.; I forgot my umbrella, so I got wet in the rain **b)** My foot slipped on the ice. I didn't fall.; My foot slipped on the ice, but I didn't fall. **c)** I might get up early tomorrow. I might sleep in.; I might get up early tomorrow, or I might sleep in.

Common Nouns and Proper Nouns, p. 42
1. b) planet **c)** street or road **d)** store or business **e)** continent **f)** ocean **g)** country
2. a) The man took a train to Regina on a rainy day. **b)** Did Wendy remember to buy jam at Westside Market? **c)** My friend said that Neptune is her favourite planet.

Exploring Proper Nouns, p. 43
1. a) Mr.Chong drove across the Peace Bridge when he visited Hamilton. **b)** My grandparents will teach me to speak Russian when they visit next January. **c)** On Mother's Day, we visited the Royal Tyrell Museum in Alberta. **d)** The Rocky Mountains stretch from Canada to the United States. **e)** Some people say English is more difficult to learn than French. **f)** Tourists visiting Ottawa often go to see the Parliament Buildings. **g)** Students at Lakeview School had a bake sale to help the United Way raise money.

Spelling Plural Nouns, pp. 44–45
1. a) windows **b)** activities **c)** lunches **d)** brushes **e)** monkeys **f)** buses **g)** taxes **h)** journeys **i)** eyes **j)** libraries **k)** holidays **l)** sixes **m)** trays **n)** beaches **o)** families **p)** addresses **q)** dishes **r)** viruses **s)** coaches **t)** islands **u)** berries **v)** boxes **w)** branches **x)** eyelashes
2. a) videos **b)** lives **c)** tomatoes **d)** pianos **e)** thieves **f)** roofs **g)** wives **h)** loaves

Possessive Nouns, p. 46
1. a) We heard the children's shouts from far away. **b)** My neighbours' house is for sale. **c)** The tiger's paws had very sharp claws. **d)** The birds' chirping woke me up early. **e)** Will the students' teacher give them homework? **f)** The women's laughter echoed down the hallway.

Action Verbs, p. 47
Underline the following verbs: **a)** exploded **b)** asked **c)** no action verb **d)** blew **e)** tripped **f)** drove **g)** no action verb **h)** flaps **i)** gave **j)** told **k)** shines **l)** no action verb

Linking Verbs, pp. 48–49
1. a) excited; an adjective **b)** upset; an adjective **c)** nurse; a noun **d)** restless; an adjective **e)** dancer; a noun
2. a) sounds **b)** tastes **c)** is **d)** become **e)** seems **f)** became **g)** feels **h)** smell

Spelling Past Tense Verbs, pp. 50–51
1. a) competed **b)** tapped **c)** climbed **d)** greeted **e)** studied **f)** stayed **g)** fixed **h)** pinned **i)** erased **j)** reached **k)** jogged **l)** warned

Past Tense of Irregular Verbs, pp. 52–53
1. a) drunk **b)** brought **c)** slept **d)** given **e)** began **f)** bitten **g)** caught **h)** come **i)** built **j)** hidden **k)** understood **l)** fed **m)** been **n)** eaten **o)** bent **p)** driven **q)** hid **r)** cut **s)** known

Using Should and Could, p. 54
1. a) could; ability in the past **b)** should; expected action b should; advice/suggestion **d)** could; possibility or might be true **e)** could; possibility or might be true **f)** should; expected action **g)** should; advice/suggestion

Using the Correct Verb Tense, p. 55
1. a) will take **b)** sprained **c)** am taking **d)** was walking **e)** understand **f)** wiAm (myll be g) sang **h)** was cutting **i)** is raining **j)** watch **k)** will play **l)** will stay
2. a) arrived **b)** cleaned **c)** tense is correct **d)** tense is correct **e)** says **f)** will be **g)** told **h)** found **i)** tense is correct **j)** said **k)** was **l)** mowed

Pronouns and Antecedents, p. 56
1. a) She **b)** them **c)** us **d)** We **e)** they **f)** I   **2. a)** it, them **b)** He, them **c)** him, her **d)** them, they, them

Adjectives Before and After Nouns, pp. 57–58
1. a) Circle "striped" and underline "sweater"; draw an arrow from "striped" to "sweater." **b)** Circle "dirty" and underline "clothes"; draw an arrow from "dirty" to "clothes." **c)** Circle "long" and underline "movie"; draw an arrow from "long" to "movie." **d)** Circle "expensive" and underline "necklace"; draw an arrow from "expensive" to "necklace." **e)** Circle "brave" and underline "woman"; draw an arrow from "brave" to "woman."
2. a) Circle "dog"; underline "fluffy" **b)** Circle "package"; underline "surprise" **c)** Circle "legs"; underline "long" **d)** Circle "thunderstorms"; underline "severe" **e)** Circle "lining"; underline "silver" **f)** Circle "mud" and underline "slippery"; circle "stream" and underline "shallow" **g)** Circle "gowns"; underline "glamorous" **h)** Circle "Alice"; underline "nervous"
3. a) Circle "Fierce," and "ancient"; underline "warriors" and "castle" **b)** Circle "old" and "hilarious"; underline "movie" **c)** Circle "shiny" and "muddy"; underline "floor" and "boots" **d)** Circle "curious" and "new"; underline "Max" and "restaurant" **e)** Circle "huge"; underline "spider" **f)** Circle "long," "sore," and "stiff"; underline "legs" **g)** Circle "Red," "white," and "huge"; underline "balloons" and "auditorium"
4. a) summer **b)** silver **c)** bravest **d)** frightened **e)** peaceful **f)** morning **g)** hungry, thirsty

Adjectives Can Describe How Many, p. 59
1. a) Circle "several"; underline "questions" **b)** Circle "each"; underline "sketches" **c)** Circle "few"; underline "people" **d)** Circle "both"; underline "hands" **e)** Circle "two"; underline "brothers" **f)** Circle "all"; underline "snakes" **g)** Circle "Most"; underline "people" **h)** Circle "Hundreds"; underline "fans" **i)** Circle "Many"; underline "children" **j)** Circle "Ten"; underline "bundles"

Demonstrative Adjectives, p. 60
1. a) Those people over by the tree are my friends. **b)** Will one of these keys in my hand open the lock? **c)** This box I'm carrying is very heavy. **d)** Please leave through that door at the end of the hall. **e)** These socks I'm wearing are very warm. **f)** That rainbow in the sky is beautiful.

Using Adjectives to Compare, pp. 61–62
1. a) nicer **b)** the tallest **c)** prettier **d)** hotter; the hottest
2. a) better **b)** the best **c)** farther **d)** worse **e)** the most **f)** the farthest **g)** more **h)** the worst **i)** better

Adverbs Can Describe How, p. 63
1. a) Circle "quietly" and underline "spoke"; draw an arrow from "quietly" to "spoke." Circle "peacefully" and underline "slept"; draw an arrow from "peacefully" to "slept." **b)** Circle "gently" and underline "laid"; draw an arrow from "gently" to "laid." Circle "silently" and underline "left"; draw an arrow from "silently" to "left." **c)** Circle "clumsily" and underline "dropped," draw an arrow from "clumsily" to "dropped"; Circle "noisily" and underline "shattered"; draw an arrow from "noisily" to "shattered." **d)** Circle "violently" and "unexpectedly"; underline "erupted"; draw arrows from "violently" and "unexpectedly" to "erupted."
2. a) Yes **b)** No **c)** Yes **d)** Yes

Adverbs Can Describe When or How Often, p. 64
a) when **b)** how often **c)** how often **d)** when **e)** when **f)** how often **g)** when, when **h)** how often **i)** when **j)** how often **k)** how often **l)** how often, how often **m)** how often, how often

Adverbs Can Describe Where, p. 65
1. a) here **b)** nearby **c)** everywhere **d)** downstairs **e)** somewhere   **2. a)** backward **b)** south **c)** forward **d)** up **e)** left, right

Exploring Adverbs That Compare, p. 66
1. a) the highest **b)** slower **c)** brighter **d)** the loudest **e)** the slowest **f)** faster **g)** higher **h)** earlier **i)** the earliest

Adverbs Can Describe Verbs, Adjectives, and Adverbs, p. 67
1. a) Circle "slightly" and draw an arrow to "annoyed." **b)** Circle "badly" and draw an arrow to "damaged." **c)** Circle "incredibly" and draw an arrow to "huge." **d)** Circle "quite" and draw an arrow to "interested." **e)** Circle "so" and draw an arrow to "helpful." **f)** Circle "awfully" and draw an arrow to "cold." **g)** Circle "really" and draw an arrow to "scary."

Punctuating Dialogue, pp. 68–69
1. a) "We've won the game!" shouted Chris. **b)** "I hope we have good weather during our vacation," Dad said. **c)** "I wonder if she noticed that we came in late," whispered Beth. **d)** "Would you like to look through the telescope?" the scientist asked. **e)** The coach said, "Now that's what I call teamwork!" f) The crowd shouted, "Don't go yet! Sing one more song!" **g)** My mom said, "I think I've seen this movie before." **h)** "This produce is all organically grown," the woman explained.
2. a) "My baby cried most of the night," said Mrs. Hernandez, "and I think it was because she had a fever." **b)** "The woman who lives next door is a doctor," explained Mr. Carson, "but she retired several years ago." **c)** "These red roses are pretty," said the gardener, "but the pink roses are even prettier!" **d)** "It has been snowing all morning," said Rita, "so I think I'll need to wear my boots when I go outside this afternoon." **e)** "My parents said you could come to the amusement park with us," said Eddie, "but will you be able to get to my house by noon?"

Write the Correct Word, p. 70
1. a) desert **b)** it's **c)** already **d)** dessert **e)** all ready **f)** it's **g)** already **h)** its

Exploring Idioms, p. 79
1. Sample answers: **a)** Tom really had to hit the books to pass his math test. **b)** Lily really hit the nail on the head when she said the chocolate cake would taste better than the white cake. **c)** My grandmother said she would move to a new house when pigs fly. **d)** Mark said he didn't want to stir up a hornet's nest by asking if there would be any homework over the holidays. **e)** Lucy was so well prepared for her audition that she was cool as a cucumber when she went on stage. **f)** Sam knew he was in hot water when he slept in late and missed the school bus. **g)** Neither Cindy nor Ann had studied for the test, so they were both in the same boat. **h)** Katy and Sandy were arguing and Tim added fuel to the fire by saying that Katy said Sandy was dumb.

Week 1, pp. 97–99

Monday   **1.** A. commutative   **2.** ●   **3.** $k = 23$ **4.** Add 9 to the previous number or $y = 9x$

Tuesday   **1.** 10   **2.** 320   **3.** A. 73 635   **4.** 1.6

Wednesday **1.** Sample answers: 3/6, 4/8   **2. a)** 1/3 **b)** 1/4   **3.** 4 2/7 < 5   **4.** 42/9

Thursday **1.** ★ (2, 7), ✚ (2, 1), ◆ (5, 4), (6, 8), (7, 3), (1, 4), (6, 2), (9, 0), (8, 7)
          2. A circle should be drawn at (4, 9).   **3.** A triangle should be drawn at (0, 5).

Friday   **1.** 1000 g; 1000 mg   **2.** B. the cube   **3.** They will hold the same amount.   **4.** 3:15 p.m.

Brain Stretch 1.56 kg

Week 2, pp. 100–102

Monday   **1.** ▦   **2.** =   **3.** ○□○○□○ ○□○□○□   **4.** Double the previous number.

Tuesday   **1.** 600 ones   **2.** 8000   **3.** =   **4.** 2.6

Wednesday **1.** Sample answers: 2/16, 3/24   **2.** >   **3.** 1 7/8   **4.**

Thursday **1.** ○ ⬠ □ ◁ ▽ ⬡ ⇨   **2.** ○ □   **3.** ⬠ ◁ ▽ ⬡ ⇨
          4. An open shape could be closed up, or a curved line could be straightened.

Friday   **1.** 10 000 kg   **2.** 250 cm   **3. a)** 1 cm^3 **b)** 6 cm^3 **c)** 8 cm^3 **4.** 12 cubic units

Brain Stretch 55 students

Week 3, pp. 103–105

Monday   **1.** C   **2.** 12   **3.** Sample answer: 1 block, 3 blocks, 5 blocks   **4.** Subtract 50 from the previous number.

Tuesday   **1. a)** 30 675 **b)** 24 012   **2. a)** 3, 30, 300, 3000 **b)** 300 000

    3. 10   **4.** 15.1

Wednesday   **1.** 1 2/3   **2.** 11/8   **3.** <   **4.** 7

Thursday   **1.** C. parallel   **2.** A, D   **3.** Accept any straight-lined closed shape with 6 sides.   **4.** None

Friday   **1.** A. 2 minutes   **2.** 445 cm   **3.** C. 18 cm^3

    4. Sample answer: No, there is still room that is not completely taken up by the cubes.

Brain Stretch   22 slices left over

Week 4, pp. 106–108

Monday   **1.** C. 2 × 5   **2.** Sample answer: 3, 9, 27 (previous number times 3)   **3.** 36, 72, 108, 144, 180   **4.** 17 + 20

Tuesday   **1.** 0.4 hundreds   **2.** thousands   **3. a)** 5, 50, 500, 5000 **b)** 9000   **4.** 1, 2, 3, 4, 6, 8, 12, 16, 24, 48

Wednesday   **1.** Sample answers: 1/2, 3/6   **2.** 20/3   **3.** 2 1/4 < 3   **4.** 155/24 or 6 $\frac{11}{24}$ bushels

Thursday   **1.** A (0, 8), B (3, 5), C (4, 7), D (4, 2), E (5, 5), F (7, 9), G (8, 4), H (9, 9), I (9, 2)

    2. The point should be at (2, 2).   **3.** The point should be at (0, 3).

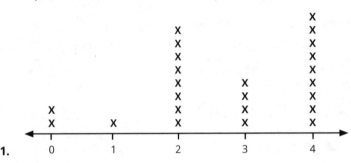

Friday   **1.**

    2. Sample answer: Most students visited the library at least twice. Two students did not go to the library at all.

Brain Stretch   The shape should be 2 units to the right and 4 units down.

Week 5, pp. 109–111

Monday   **1.** m = 12   **2.** Sample answer: 10 blocks, 8 blocks, 6 blocks   **3.** Alternate between add 6, then add 4.

    4. 56

Tuesday   **1. a)** The 2 in 742 represents 2 ones. **b)** The 2 in 724 represents 2 tens or 20. **2.** $9.55 **3.** 23, 109, 567, 876

    4. 60.74

Wednesday   **1.** 1/2   **2.** >   **3. a)** 3/4 **b)** 2/10 or 1/5   **4.** It is equidistant from 1 and 1/2.

Thursday   **1.** A. intersecting   **2.** Accept any two closed figures with more than 4 straight sides.   **3.** quadrilateral

    4. A. parallelogram, B. rhombus, and C. quadrilateral

Friday   **1.** 1200 months   **2.** 20 dm   **3.** 272 cm perimeter and 4480 cm^2 area   **4.** 5 cubic units

Brain Stretch   7:40 a.m.

Week 6, pp. 112–114

Monday   **1.** Sample answer: 67, 65, 63, 61   **2.** 1, 11, 4, 8, 2   **3.** C, C   **4. a)** z = 016 **b)** y = 11

Tuesday   **1. a)** 34 **b)** 340 **c)** 34 000 **d)** Sample answer: For each zero in the power of 10, there is one zero in the product.   **2.** A. $9.95   **3.** 5   **4.** <

Wednesday   **1.** Sample answers: 8/14, 12/21   **2.** 9/4 < 12/4   **3.** 3/2 and 1 1/2   **4.** 4/3 is greater

Thursday   **1.** *A* (1, 3), *B* (2, 7), *C* (3, 5), *D* (4, 2), *E* (6, 8), *F* (7, 9), *G* (7, 4), *H* (9, 8), *I* (9, 3)   **2.** A point should be drawn at (0, 0).   **3.** A point should be drawn at (8, 1).

Friday   **1.** metres or kilometres   **2. a)** 3000 m **b)** 1500 mm **c)** 800 cm   **3.** 16 800 m   **4.** 9 cubic units

Brain Stretch   **a)** acute **b)** straight **c)** obtuse **d)** acute **e)** obtuse **f)** obtuse **g)** right **h)** straight

Week 7, pp. 115–117

Monday   **1. a)** 8 **b)** 18   **2.** 63, 54, 90, 99, 36   **3.** previous number times 2   **4.** 62 > 60

Tuesday   **1.** 900 ones   **2. a)** 80 000 + 7000 + 400 + 50 + 1   **b)** 10 000 + 8000 + 300 + 80   **3.** =   **4.** 55

Wednesday   **1.** 7/9   **2.** 9/4 < 12/4   **3. a)** 4.3 **b)** 2.5 **c)** 0.4   **4.** 3 3/4 cups

Thursday   **1. a)** sphere, 0, 0, 0   **b)** cylinder, 3, 2, 0   **c)** rectangular prism, 6, 12, 8   **d)** cone, 2, 1, 1

Friday   **1.** 10   **2.** 5   **3.** Chris   **4.** They planted the same number of tulips.

Brain Stretch   480 m³

Week 8, pp. 118–120

Monday   **1.** D. 6 × (40 + 2)   **2.** Output = input × 11; 66, 99   **3.** =   **4.** 75 – 25

Tuesday   **1.** 200   **2.** $100   **3.** 0.06   **4.** 2700

Wednesday   **1.** Sample answers: 5/11, 20/44   **2.** 41/8   **3.** =   **4.** 1/6

Thursday   **1.** A: 6 sides, B: 3 sides, C: 5 sides, D: 4 sides, E: 4 sides, F: 8 sides, G: 3 sides, H: 4 sides, I: 4 sides, J: 4 sides   **2.** Quadrilaterals: D, E, J; Not Quadrilaterals: A, B, C, F, G, H, and I.

Friday   **1.** 45 minutes   **2. a)** 3600 m   **b)** 18 000 m   **3.** 34.6 units   **4.** 20 cubic units

Brain Stretch   **a)** B   **b)** A

Week 9, pp. 121–123

Monday   **1. a)** *r* = 2 **b)** *x* = 49   **2. c)** ◁   **3.** 3 times larger   **4.** (12 + 8) ÷ 2

Tuesday   **1.** 40 tens   **2. a)** 1/10 of the 4 to the left **b)** 10 times the 4 to the right   **3.** <   **4.** 784

Wednesday   **1.** 2 6/9   **2.** 29/30   **3.** 19/4 < 20/4   **4.** 2, 2/10

Thursday   **1. A.** intersecting and **B.** perpendicular   **2.** Both have 4 straight sides and 2 pairs of parallel sides.   **3. B.** equilateral, **C.** triangle   **4.** congruent

Friday   **1. a)** 125 mm **b)** 405 mm   **2.** 112.5 words   **3.** Room A: area: 40 units; perimeter: 96 m²; Room B: perimeter: 36 units; area: 91 m²; Room A has larger area and perimeter.   **4. a)** 7 cubic units **b)** 28 cubic units

Brain Stretch   19°C

Week 10, pp. 124–126

Monday   **1. a)** *r* = 8 **b)** *x* = 6   **2.** 90, 120, 10, 30, 60   **3.** (6 + 5) × 3   **4.** D. 8 × 2

Tuesday   **1.** 100 ten thousands   **2. a)** 300 **b)** 3000 **c)** 10   **3. a)** 7; 7.3 **b)** 1; 0.9   **4.** 7.1

Wednesday   **1.** 13/45   **2.** 1 1/6 < 2   **3. a)** 1.33, 3.65, 3.94 **b)** 0.25, 0.5, 0.99   **4.** 14 cm

Thursday **1.**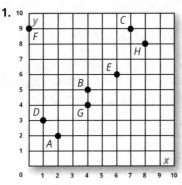

2. a) *B, G* **b)** *C, F* **3.** None

Friday **1.** Chocolate: 10 scoops, Chocolate chip: 18 scoops, Strawberry: 24 scoops, Vanilla: 14 scoops

2. mean = 16.5; range: 24 – 10 = 14 **3.** A. line graph

Brain Stretch **1.** bar graph **2.** circle graph **3.** bar graph **4.** line graph **5.** circle graph **6.** line graph

Week 11, pp. 127–129

Monday **1. a)** 3 **b)** 28 **c)** 24 **2.** output = input × 100; 800, 1000, 11 **3.** (8 + 56) ÷ 4 **4.** (16 + 4) x (8 – 1) = 140

Tuesday **1.** Sample answer: 6999 **2. a)** 96 521 **b)** 12 569 **3.** 4.2 < 4.5 **4.** 5856

Wednesday **1.** Sample answers: 6/10, 12/20 **2.** 1 1/13 **3.** 3 cm² **4.** No, she has only 14.8 m, so she is missing 1.2 m of fabric.

Thursday **1.** A. octagon **2.** A. acute, D. scalene **3.** 2 **4.** similar

Friday **1.** a) continuous b) discrete c) discrete **2.** Sample answer: **a)** height b) the number of people in a bus

3. a) first-hand **b)** second-hand **4. a)** first-hand **b)** second-hand

Brain Stretch Honey Hoops, because Fruity Flakes cost $2.75/500 g (0.55 x 5 = 2.75).

Week 12, pp. 130–132

Monday **1.** B. 24 × 10 **2. a)** 111116 **b)** C. growing **3.** (11 – 5) + 2 **4. a)** 56 **b)** 9

Tuesday **1. a)** 0; 0.3 **b)** 4, 4.1 **2.** 2.9 < 3.9 **3.** 63.6 **4.** 44

Wednesday **1.** 9 3/6 or 9 1/2 **2.** 6/7 **3.** closer to 0 **4.** 0.4

Thursday **1. quadrilaterals:** A, B, C, E, F, H **parallelograms:** B, C, E, H **2.** D, G

Friday **1. a)** 12 **b)** 6 **c)** 6 **d)** 10 **e)** 11 **f)** continuous

Brain Stretch 246 cm = 2.46 m < 3.6 m. George's plane can fly farther. The difference is 114 cm.

Week 13, pp. 133–135

Monday **a)** 1, 3, 5, 7, 9; 1, 4, 7, 10, 13 **b)** the only similar numbers are prime numbers **2. a)** 20 **b)** 40 **3.** *b* + 11

Tuesday **1.** 30 **2.** a) 73 082 b) 80 512 **3.** 0.99 > 0.09 **4.** 31.5

Wednesday **1.** 13/14 **2.** 14/5 **3.** 2/7 **4.** 1 3/4

Thursday **1. a)** triangular prism, 5, 9, 6 **B.** cube, 6, 12, 6 **C.** square pyramid, 5, 8, 5

Friday **1.** a) 50 mm b) 132 mm **2.** C. metres **3.** about 210 m **4.** a) 12 cubic units b) 36 cubic units

Brain Stretch 3/8, $11.25

Week 14, pp. 136–138

Monday **1. a)** 0, 2, 4, 6, 8 **b)** 0, 1, 2, 3, 4 **2.** (0, 0) (2, 1) (4, 2) (6, 3) (8, 4) **3.** If the points are plotted correctly, students should be able to draw a straight line diagonally out of the point (0, 0).

Tuesday **1.** 1000 **2.** hundredths **3.** 9.6 = 9.6 **4.** 32 896 **5.** 76 099, 76 101

Wednesday   **1.** 19/14 or 1 5/14   **2.** 23/4   **3.** 1 > 1/5   **4.**

Thursday   **1.** B. quadrilateral, C. square, D. parallelogram   **2.** A and B are trapezoids   **3.** The polygon should have 5 sides and be irregular.   **4.** scalene or isoceles triangles have no right angles

Friday   **1.** 175, 100, 125, 225   **2.** Saturday   **3.** 225 – 100 = 125   **4.** 100 tickets   **5.** Sample answer: Number of Tickets Sold by Day for Elmwood School's Play

Brain Stretch   1 1/3 = 4/3, so half is 2/3 cup. Luke should use 2/3 cup sugar for half the recipe.

Week 15, pp. 139–141

Monday   **1. a)** 9 **b)** 1   **2.** (5 + 7) × (2 + 3)   **3. a)** C **b)** P   **4.** 27 = 3 × 9; 9 = 3 × 3. Prime factorization: 3 × 3 × 3.

Tuesday   **1.** 200   **2. a)** 30 000 **b)** 30   **3.** 30   **4.** 18.62

Wednesday   **1.** 2 2/16 or 2 1/8   **2.** 1/4   **3.** 2, 3, 4, 5   **4.** 3 1/4

Thursday   **1.** rotation   **2.** drawing should show translation   **3.** drawing should show rotation   **4.** drawing should show reflection

Friday   **1.** heads or tails   **2.** HH, HT, TH, TT; 4 possible outcomes   **3. a)** 3/5 **b)** 2/5 **c)** 3/5   **4.** 1/4

Brain Stretch   8:23 a.m.

Week 16, pp. 141–144

Monday   **1. a)** 12, 11, 10, 9, 8; 12, 9, 6, 3, 0 **b)** It's just like counting back by 1 and 3.   **2.** 14 **3.** (16 ÷ 8) + 43

Tuesday   **1.** $6.00 + $17.00 = $23.00   **2.** 4   **3.** 0.62 < 2.9   **4.** 60 000 + 7000 + 300 + 90 + 8

Wednesday   **1.** 14 3/4 or 59/4   **2.** 50/15 > 36/15 **3.** a) 28/100 b) 1 67/100 c) 9/10   **4.** 4

Thursday   **1.**

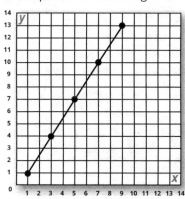

2. no parallel sides: B, C, E; 1 pair of parallel sides: F; 2 pairs of parallel sides: A, D, G

Friday: **1.** There should be 3 more Xs in the 4 and 4 1/2 columns and one more in the 2 column.   **2.** 47 nails altogether   **3.** Yes, he has enough.   **4.** No, he is missing five 5-cm nails.

Brain Stretch   Sample answer: 5 x 6, 3 x 10

Week 17, pp. 145–147

Monday   **1. a)** 1, 3, 5, 7, 9 **b)** 1, 4, 7, 10, 13   **2.** (1, 1), (3, 4), (5, 7), (7, 10), (9, 13)

3. The points lie on a straight line.

Tuesday   **1.** 60 000   **2.** $11.35 **3.** 0.8 < 0.9   **4.** 98 776.42

Wednesday   **1.** 3 1/4   **2.** 17/6 or 2 5/6   **3.** 7/2, 3 1/2   **4.** 6 students were absent

Thursday **1.** at the bakery **2.** Go 4 blocks north, then 2 blocks west. **3.** Students' routes will vary.

Friday **1.** 9000 g **2.** 200 **3.** George's plane can fly farther. The difference is 120 cm. **4.** 5 cubic metres

Brain Stretch Sample answers: 7 dimes, or 6 dimes and 2 nickels. The fewest number of coins she could receive is 2 quarters and 2 dimes.

Week 18, pp. 148–150

Monday **1. a)** $(50 - 40) \times 8$ **2. a)** 11 **b)** 270 **3.** 2 times smaller **4.** 90 years old

Tuesday **1.** 35 000 **2.** 1, 3, 9, 27 **3.** 13.3 **4.** $7.00 **5. a)** $0.40 **b)** $0.40

Wednesday **1.** 1 **2.** closer to 1/2 **3.** = **4.** 31 1/2

Thursday **1.** B. quadrilateral, D. trapezoid **2.** C. equilateral **3.** Students' drawings will vary **4.** similar

Friday **1.** A. grams **2.** 21 L per week; 42 L in 2 weeks **3.** Perimeter: 32 m; Area: 28 square units **4.** 48 cubic metres

Brain Stretch No, he spent 3/5 of his savings on the game.

Week 19, pp. 151–153

Monday **1. a)** 4, 6, 8, 10, 12; 0, 2, 4, 6, 8 **b)** It's just like counting on by 2. **2.** $(3 + 16) \times 5$ **3.** 75

Tuesday **1.** 70 **2.** 20 000 **3.** 2 **4.** 7.04

Wednesday **1.** 1 5/12 **2.** 11 1/2 **3.** 1/4, 1/2, 5/8, 3/4 **4.** $1.00

Thursday **1.** Bakery (2, 2); Bank (11, 8); Flower shop (7, 6); Gas station (6, 1); Pet store (12, 5); Restaurant (3, 9)

Friday **1.** 222 boxes of cookies altogether **2.** $444 **3.** 14 students received a prize

Brain Stretch **a)** $l = 3w + 8$ **b)** $2w + 2(3w + 8)$

Week 20, pp. 154–156

Monday **1. a)** 4, 6, 8, 10, 12 **b)** 0, 2, 4, 6, 8 **2.** (4, 0) (6, 2) (8, 4) (10, 6) (12, 8) **3.** The points make a straight line.

Tuesday **1.** 57 **2. a)** $2.00 **b)** $2.00 **3.** 61.47 **4.** 6720

Wednesday **1.** 98/11 **2.** 12 3/7 **3.** closer to 0 **4.** 1/8 kg for each loaf

Thursday **1.** A. parallelogram, B. 4 sides, C. quadrilateral, D. rhombus **2.** Shapes will vary, but should have only one pair of parallel sides. **3.** B. scalene, C. right, D. acute **4.** 5 lines of symmetry

Friday **1.** 6700 mL **2. a)** length: 3 cm; width: 3 cm; height: 4 cm **b)** 36 cubic centimetres **3. a)** 14:00 **b)** 07:15 **c)** 23:35 **4.** 12 cubic metres

Brain Stretch **a)** They made 30 cups of lemonade. **b)** No, there won't be enough. If 20 students had 3 cups of lemonade each, they would need 60 cups, but they only have 30 cups.

Multiplication Fact Fun, p. 159
1. 0 **2.** 30 **3.** 0 **4.** 56 **5.** 9 **6.** 1 **7.** 6 **8.** 54 **9.** 32 **10.** 10 **11.** 42 **12.** 8 **13.** 0 **14.** 40 **15.** 14 **16.** 6 **17.** 0 **18.** 80 **19.** 72 **20.** 21 **21.** 28 **22.** 36 **23.** 100 **24.** 20 **25.** 30 **26.** 12 **27.** 3 **28.** 12 **29.** 72 **30.** 35 **31.** 4 **32.** 48 **33.** 40 **34.** 25 **35.** 24 **36.** 15 **37.** 28 **38.** 18 **39.** 45 **40.** 40 **41.** 2 **42.** 24 **43.** 7 **44.** 8 **45.** 20 **46.** 9 **47.** 42 **48.** 18 **49.** 64 **50.** 16 **51.** 4 **52.** 0 **53.** 21 **54.** 35 **55.** 18 **56.** 5 **57.** 10 **58.** 90 **59.** 81 **60.** 0

Multiplying by Multiples of 10, 100, 1000, and 10 000, p. 160
1. a) 6, 60, 600, 6000, 60 000 **b)** 32, 320, 3200, 32 000, 320 000 **c)** 5, 50, 500, 5000, 50 000 **d)** 48, 480, 4800, 48 000, 480 000 **e)** 45, 450, 4500, 45 000, 450 000 **f)** 24, 240, 2400, 24 000, 240 000 **g)** 42, 420, 4200, 42 000, 420 000 **h)** 6, 60, 600, 6000, 60 000 **i)** 15, 150, 1500, 15 000, 150 000

Multiplication by Multiples of 10, 100, 1000, and 10 000, p. 161
1. 140 **2.** 800 **3.** 30 000 **4.** 60 000 **5.** 320 **6.** 7000 **7.** 2700 **8.** 2500 **9.** 70 000 **10.** 810 **11.** 600 **12.** 20 000 **13.** 240 **14.** 6400 **15.** 90 000 **16.** 600 **17.** 210 **18.** 10 000 **19.** 210 000 **20.** 6300 **21.** 8000 **22.** 42 000 **23.** 480 **24.** 16 000 **25.** 6000 **26.** 180 **27.** 540 000 **28.** 1500 **29.** 160 **30.** 8000 **31.** 600 **32.** 250 **33.** 280 000 **34.** 4000 **35.** 160 **36.** 1200 **37.** 2000 **38.** 4000 **39.** 900 **40.** 1000

Multiplying Two-Digit Numbers by One-Digit Numbers, p. 162
1. 174   **2.** 365   **3.** 108   **4.** 288   **5.** 168   **6.** 188   **7.** 95   **8.** 182   **9.** 220   **10.** 243   **11.** 450   **12.** 784

Multiplying Two-Digit Numbers by Two-Digit Numbers, p. 163
1. 754   **2.** 3285   **3.** 918   **4.** 928   **5.** 1428   **6.** 2068   **7.** 665   **8.** 442   **9.** 770   **10.** 2673   **11.** 2700   **12.** 2744

Multiplying Multi-Digit Numbers by One-Digit Numbers, pp. 164–165
1. 1866   **2.** 1752   **3.** 6776   **4.** 4878   **5.** 694   **6.** 2455   **7.** 5586   **8.** 740   **9.** 6534   **10.** 1575   **11.** 1960   **12.** 1586   **13.** 2775   **14.** 2632   **15.** 2163   **16.** 3776   **17.** 1710   **18.** 1041   **19.** 2608   **20.** 1158   **21.** 13 401   **22.** 55 431   **23.** 13 640   **24.** 37 084   **25.** 41 984   **26.** 24 647   **27.** 13 914   **28.** 57 728

Estimating a Product, pp. 166–167
1. a) round 57 to 60, 70 × 60 = 4200
b) round 44 to 40, 9 × 40 = 360
c) round 316 to 300, 7 × 300 = 2100
d) round 85 to 90, 5 × 90 = 450
e) round 32 to 30, 10 × 30 = 300
f) round 65 to 70, 60 × 70 = 4200
g) round 28 to 30, 11 × 30 = 330
h) round 79 to 80, 4 × 80 = 240
i) round 93 to 90, 30 × 90 = 2700
2. a) round 34 to 30 and 29 to 30, 30 × 30 = 900
b) round 67 to 70 and 63 to 60, 70 × 60 = 4200
c) round 83 to 80 and 87 to 90, 80 × 90 = 7200
d) round 81 to 80 and 39 to 40, 80 × 40 = 3200
e) round 26 to 30 and 31 to 30, 30 × 30 = 900
f) round 98 to 100 and 18 to 20, 100 × 20 = 2000
g) round 53 to 50 and 546 to 500, 50 × 500 = 25 000
h) round 12 to 10 and 110 to 100, 10 × 100 = 1000
i) round 36 to 40 and 791 to 800, 40 × 800 = 32 000

Division Fact Fun, p. 168
1. 6   **2.** 2   **3.** 6   **4.** 10   **5.** 0   **6.** 7   **7.** 6   **8.** 4   **9.** 3   **10.** 7   **11.** 7   **12.** 2   **13.** 3   **14.** 10   **15.** 10   **16.** 10   **17.** 7   **18.** 6   **19.** 3   **20.** 6   **21.** 3   **22.** 8   **23.** 6   **24.** 9   **25.** 8   **26.** 1   **27.** 1   **28.** 7   **29.** 0   **30.** 2   **31.** 7   **32.** 6   **33.** 5   **34.** 9   **35.** 0   **36.** 7   **37.** 4   **38.** 5   **39.** 8   **40.** 2   **41.** 8   **42.** 8   **43.** 7   **44.** 5   **45.** 6   **46.** 7   **47.** 8   **48.** 9   **49.** 8   **50.** 9   **51.** 2   **52.** 3   **53.** 4   **54.** 10   **55.** 0   **56.** 0   **57.** 4   **58.** 2   **59.** 9   **60.** 9

Dividing Multiples of 10, 100, 1000, and 10 000, p. 169
1. a) 2, 20, 200, 2000, 20 000 **b)** 6, 60, 600, 6000, 60 000 **c)** 1, 10, 100, 1000, 10 000 **d)** 1, 10, 100, 1000, 10 000 **e)** 5, 50, 500, 5000, 50 000 **f)** 7, 70, 700, 7000, 70 000

Division of Multiples of 10, 100, 1000, and 10 000, p. 170
1. 10   **2.** 180   **3.** 1500   **4.** 20   **5.** 100   **6.** 60   **7.** 70   **8.** 1200   **9.** 7000   **10.** 1   **11.** 1000   **12.** 600   **13.** 70   **14.** 10   **15.** 120   **16.** 8   **17.** 700   **18.** 100   **19.** 90   **20.** 600   **21.** 5   **22.** 400   **23.** 6000   **24.** 800   **25.** 100   **26.** 9   **27.** 10   **28.** 1000   **29.** 70   **30.** 12 000   **31.** 11 000   **32.** 110   **33.** 400   **34.** 3000   **35.** 20   **36.** 50   **37.** 40 000   **38.** 5   **39.** 5   **40.** 30

Dividing Two-Digit Numbers by One-Digit Numbers, p. 171
1. 7   **2.** 31   **3.** 39   **4.** 3 R 2   **5.** 13 R 1   **6.** 8   **7.** 39 R 1   **8.** 3 R 1   **9.** 17 R 2   **10.** 17 R 3   **11.** 14 R 5   **12.** 12 R 2

Dividing Multi-Digit Numbers by One-Digit Numbers, p. 172
1. 121   **2.** 183   **3.** 450   **4.** 311   **5.** 38 R 3   **6.** 19 R 5   **7.** 404 R 1   **8.** 72 R 1   **9.** 116 R 3   **10.** 45   **11.** 65 R 1   **12.** 307 R 2

Dividing Multi-Digit Numbers, p. 173
1. 321   **2.** 106   **3.** 333   **4.** 97   **5.** 181   **6.** 185   **7.** 308   **8.** 183   **9.** 76   **10.** 23   **11.** 49

Outstanding Effort!

Grade 5 Certificate of Merit

_____